Jarmark

33 1/3 Global

33 1/3 Global, a series related to but independent from **33 1/3**, takes the format of the original series of short, music-based books and brings the focus to music throughout the world. With initial volumes focusing on Japanese and Brazilian music, the series will also include volumes on the popular music of Australia/Oceania, Europe, Africa, the Middle East, and more.

33 1/3 Japan

Series Editor: Noriko Manabe

Spanning a range of artists and genres—from the 1970s rock of Happy End to technopop band Yellow Magic Orchestra, the Shibuya-kei of Cornelius, classic anime series *Cowboy Bebop*, J-Pop/EDM hybrid Perfume, and vocaloid star Hatsune Miku—**33 1/3 Japan** is a series devoted to in-depth examination of Japanese popular music of the twentieth and twenty-first centuries.

Published Titles:
Supercell's *Supercell* by Keisuke Yamada
AKB48 by Patrick W. Galbraith and Jason G. Karlin
Yoko Kanno's *Cowboy Bebop Soundtrack* by Rose Bridges
Perfume's *Game* by Patrick St. Michel
Cornelius's *Fantasma* by Martin Roberts
Joe Hisaishi's *My Neighbor Totoro: Soundtrack* by Kunio Hara
Shonen Knife's *Happy Hour* by Brooke McCorkle
Nenes' *Koza Dabasa* by Henry Johnson
Yuming's *The 14th Moon* by Lasse Lehtonen
Kohaku utagassen: The Red and White Song Contest by Shelley Brunt
Toshiko Akiyoshi-Lew Tabackin Big Band's *Kogun* by E. Taylor Atkins
S.O.B.'s *Don't Be Swindle* by Mahon Murphy and Ran Zwigenberg

Forthcoming Titles:
Yellow Magic Orchestra's *Yellow Magic Orchestra* by Toshiyuki Ohwada

33 1/3 Brazil

Series Editor: Jason Stanyek

Covering the genres of samba, tropicália, rock, hip hop, forró, bossa nova, heavy metal and funk, among others, **33 1/3 Brazil** is a series devoted to in-depth examination of the most important Brazilian albums of the twentieth and twenty-first centuries.

Published Titles:
Caetano Veloso's *A Foreign Sound* by Barbara Browning
Tim Maia's *Tim Maia Racional Vols. 1 &2* by Allen Thayer
João Gilberto and Stan Getz's *Getz/Gilberto* by Brian McCann
Gilberto Gil's *Refazenda* by Marc A. Hertzman
Dona Ivone Lara's *Sorriso Negro* by Mila Burns
Milton Nascimento and Lô Borges's *The Corner Club* by Jonathon Grasse
Racionais MCs' *Sobrevivendo no Inferno* by Derek Pardue
Naná Vasconcelos's *Saudades* by Daniel B. Sharp
Chico Buarque's First *Chico Buarque* by Charles A. Perrone

Forthcoming titles:
Jorge Ben Jor's *África Brasil* by Frederick J. Moehn

33 1/3 Europe

Series Editor: Fabian Holt

Spanning a range of artists and genres, **33 1/3 Europe** offers engaging accounts of popular and culturally significant albums of Continental Europe and the North Atlantic from the twentieth and twenty-first centuries.

Published Titles:
Darkthrone's *A Blaze in the Northern Sky* by Ross Hagen
Ivo Papazov's *Balkanology* by Carol Silverman
Heiner Müller and Heiner Goebbels's *Wolokolamsker Chaussee* by Philip V. Bohlman
Modeselektor's *Happy Birthday!* by Sean Nye

Mercyful Fate's *Don't Break the Oath* by Henrik Marstal
Bea Playa's *I'll Be Your Plaything* by Anna Szemere and András Rónai
Various Artists' *DJs do Guetto* by Richard Elliott
Czesław Niemen's *Niemen Enigmatic* by Ewa Mazierska and Mariusz Gradowski
Massada's *Astaganaga* by Lutgard Mutsaers
Los Rodriguez's *Sin Documentos* by Fernán del Val and Héctor Fouce
Édith Piaf's *Récital 1961* by David Looseley
Nuovo Canzoniere Italiano's *Bella Ciao* by Jacopo Tomatis
Iannis Xenakis's *Persepolis* by Aram Yardumian
Vopli Vidopliassova's *Tantsi* by Maria Sonevytsky
Amália Rodrigues's *Amália at the Olympia* by Lila Ellen Gray
Ardit Gjebrea's *Projekt Jon* by Nicholas Tochka
Aqua's *Aquarium* by C.C. McKee
J.M.K.E.'s *To the Cold Land* by Brigitta Davidjants
Taco Hemingway's *Jarmark* by Kamila Rymajdo

Forthcoming Titles:
Tripes' *Kefali Gemato Hrisafi* by Dafni Tragaki
Silly's *Februar* by Michael Rauhut
CCCP's *Fedeli Alla Linea's 1964-1985 Affinità-Divergenze Fra Il Compagno Togliatti E Noi Del Conseguimento Della Maggiore Età* by Giacomo Bottà

33 1/3 Oceania

Series Editors: Jon Stratton (senior editor) and Jon Dale (specializing in books on albums from Aotearoa/New Zealand)

Spanning a range of artists and genres from Australian Indigenous artists to Maori and Pasifika artists, from Aotearoa/New Zealand noise music to Australian rock, and including music from Papua and other Pacific islands, 33 1/3 Oceania offers exciting accounts of albums that illustrate the wide range of music made in the Oceania region.

Published Titles:
John Farnham's *Whispering Jack* by Graeme Turner
The Church's *Starfish* by Chris Gibson
Regurgitator's *Unit* by Lachlan Goold and Lauren Istvandity
Kylie Minogue's *Kylie* by Adrian Renzo and Liz Giuffre
Alastair Riddell's *Space Waltz* by Ian Chapman
Hunters & Collectors's *Human Frailty* by Jon Stratton
The Front Lawn's *Songs from the Front Lawn* by Matthew Bannister
Bic Runga's *Drive* by Henry Johnson
The Dead C's *Clyma est mort* by Darren Jorgensen
Ed Kuepper's *Honey Steel's Gold* by John Encarnacao
Chain's *Toward the Blues* by Peter Beilharz
Hilltop Hoods' *The Calling* by Dianne Rodger
Screamfeeder's *Kitten Licks* by Ben Green and Ian Rogers
The Triffids' *Born Sandy Devotional* by Christina Ballico
Soundtrack from *Saturday Night Fever* by Clinton Walker
5MMM's *Compilation Album of Adelaide Bands 1980* by Collette Snowden
The Clean's *Boodle Boodle Boodle* by Geoff Stahl
The Avalanches' *Since I Left You* by Charles Fairchild
John Sangster's *Lord of the Rings, Vols. 1–3* by Bruce Johnson

Forthcoming Titles:
INXS' *Kick* by Ryan Daniel and Lauren Moxey
Crowded House's *Together Alone* by Barnaby Smith
Sunnyboys' *Sunnyboys* by Stephen Bruel
Eyeliner's *BUY NOW* by Michael Brown
silverchair's *Frogstomp* by Jay Daniel Thompson
TISM's *Machiavelli and the Four Seasons* by Tyler Jenke
The La De Das' *The Happy Prince* by John Tebbutt
Gary Shearston's *Dingo* by Peter Mills

Jarmark

Kamila Rymajdo

Series Editor: Fabian Holt

BLOOMSBURY ACADEMIC
NEW YORK • LONDON • OXFORD • NEW DELHI • SYDNEY

BLOOMSBURY ACADEMIC
Bloomsbury Publishing Inc, 1385 Broadway, New York, NY 10018, USA
Bloomsbury Publishing Plc, 50 Bedford Square, London, WC1B 3DP, UK
Bloomsbury Publishing Ireland, 29 Earlsfort Terrace, Dublin 2, D02 AY28, Ireland

BLOOMSBURY, BLOOMSBURY ACADEMIC and the Diana logo are trademarks of
Bloomsbury Publishing Plc

First published in the United States of America 2025
Reprinted 2025 (twice)

Copyright © Kamila Rymajdo, 2025

All rights reserved. No part of this publication may be: i) reproduced or transmitted in any form, electronic or mechanical, including photocopying, recording or by means of any information storage or retrieval system without prior permission in writing from the publishers; or ii) used or reproduced in any way for the training, development or operation of artificial intelligence (AI) technologies, including generative AI technologies. The rights holders expressly reserve this publication from the text and data mining exception as per Article 4(3) of the Digital Single Market Directive (EU) 2019/790.

Bloomsbury Publishing Inc does not have any control over, or responsibility for, any third-party websites referred to or in this book. All internet addresses given in this book were correct at the time of going to press. The author and publisher regret any inconvenience caused if addresses have changed or sites have ceased to exist, but can accept no responsibility for any such changes.

Whilst every effort has been made to locate copyright holders the publishers would be grateful to hear from any person(s) not here acknowledged.

Library of Congress Cataloging-in-Publication Data
Names: Rymajdo, Kamila, author.
Title: Jarmark / Kamila Rymajdo.
Other titles: Taco Hemingway's Jarmark
Description: [1.] | New York: Bloomsbury Academic, 2025. | Series: 33 1/3
Europe | Includes bibliographical references.
Identifiers: LCCN 2024029049 (print) | LCCN 2024029050 (ebook) |
ISBN 9798765103067 (paperback) | ISBN 9798765103050 (hardback) |
ISBN 9798765103074 (ebook) | ISBN 9798765103081 (pdf)
Subjects: LCSH: Hemingway, Taco. Jarmark. | Rap (Music)–Poland–History
and criticism. | Rap (Music)–Political aspects–Poland.
Classification: LCC ML420.H366 R96 2025 (print) | LCC ML420.H366 (ebook) |
DDC 782.421649092–dc23/eng/20240705
LC record available at https://lccn .loc .gov /2024029049
LC ebook record available at https://lccn .loc .gov /2024029050

ISBN: HB: 979-8-7651-0305-0
PB: 979-8-7651-0306-7
ePDF: 979-8-7651-0308-1
eBook: 979-8-7651-0307-4

Series: 33 1/3 Europe

Typeset by Deanta Global Publishing Services, Chennai, India
Printed and bound in Great Britain

For product safety related questions contact productsafety@bloomsbury.com.

To find out more about our authors and books visit www.bloomsbury.com
and sign up for our newsletters.

Contents

Introduction: What is Polish Hip Hop? 1

1 **Poland's postsocialist history and the rise of Taco Hemingway** 15

2 **The textual analysis of *Jarmark*** 49

3 **Social remittances, the reception of the album and the failure of the 'Grand Narrative' of Polish migration** 87

Bibliography 109
Index 122

Introduction
What is Polish Hip Hop?

In the summer of 2022 when I was just starting my research for this book, I bumped into a videographer at the airport in Manchester, United Kingdom, where I live. He was going to Warsaw to film Polish-British rappers collaborating with rappers in Poland and felt hopeful about the growing ties between scenes in the two countries. He felt that young Polish-British rappers, usually children of those who emigrated after the 2004 EU enlargement, saw the Polish scene as a hotbed of opportunity that they might not have back home in the United Kingdom. Prominent emigree rappers with Polish heritage have made it big in Poland in recent years, including Malik Montana and Mr. Polska, who returned to Poland after some years of relative success in Holland. This trajectory can also be found in the career of the subject of this book, Taco Hemingway, who moved to the United Kingdom to study anthropology, then tried to launch a rap career while there. He failed in the United Kingdom but found overnight success upon his return to Poland with his debut Polish EP, *Trójkąt warszawski* (*Warsaw triangle*). Eventually, Hemingway became the first Polish artist to be streamed a billion times on Spotify (Korycka 2021).

The international media industry's neglect of local rappers is not a problem exclusive to Poland. There are scant examples of Eastern European rap making it on the world stage. It is also not a problem singular to Eastern Europeans. Even British rappers have traditionally found it difficult to break the American market, and it is only with the worldwide appetite for grime in the late 2010s and endorsements from heavyweights such as Canadian superstar Drake that British artists like Skepta and Giggs have gained recognition in the United States and beyond. However, one could argue that in a landscape where a Spanish-language rapper like Bad Bunny is in the top five most-streamed artists at the time of writing in 2023 and the top ten is made up of acts from seven different countries (Page and Dalla Riva 2023: 23), there should be possibility for even Polish rappers to have a chance.

Why has Polish popular music failed in global markets in the past? The general explanation in global theory of popular music is that small non-English-speaking countries have faced cultural barriers and been exploited as sources of exotic sounds by the international industry (Wallis and Malm 1984). In the Eastern European context, the promotion of music on the international stage after 1989 faced challenges due to the connotations attached to the region's communist history and its subsequent demise (Elavsky 2011: 6). Paradoxically, these works were no longer perceived as exotic or representative of oppressed cultures, nor were they considered central enough to embody a pan-European perspective. Moreover, the shift in global power dynamics post-communism, moving from East–West Cold War dynamics to a North–South economic divide, further marginalized Eastern music scenes (Mazierska and Goddard 2014: 9–10). As such, within music, the artists and scenes of Latin America or South Korea have increasingly been garnering international audiences, while those from Eastern Europe have not. Still, as the career of Taco Hemingway illustrates, perhaps it is enough, even desirable, to be a star in your own country only. Much of Hemingway's output focuses on his frustration with being famous and constantly followed by paparazzi. But, as he attests through his songwriting, Hemingway is able to escape by spending much of his time travelling outside Poland, where no one knows who he is.

As such, Hemingway's career also reflects the long history of Polish artists in exile, from poets such as Adam Mickiewicz to film director Roman Polanski. This book will therefore also analyse *Jarmark* (*Fair*) in the context of postcolonial and migration studies of Eastern Europe. I ask whether because he has lived abroad, Taco Hemingway positions himself as a colonial or postcolonial subject. Is he a victim of the marginal position of Polish emigrants in the West,[1] shaped by the

---

[1] The West is both a geographical and cultural concept. It might designate the region which is located west of the place one's occupies, as well as a specific set of heritages, social norms and aesthetic values, adopted by people with historical ties to European countries and to the variety of cultures within Europe itself, with roots in Greco-Roman civilization and Christianity. In the Polish and Eastern European context, the West essentially meant the countries on the west of the Berlin Wall or so called Iron Curtain. It also included countries which adopted capitalism and representative (parliamentary) democracy, irrespective of their precise geographical location. From this perspective, in Poland Japan could be described as a western country, despite being geographically on the east of Poland, on account of its political and economic system.

The West and 'western' are also relative concepts, in a sense that some phenomena could be described as more western than others. Such hierarchy pertains especially to popular music, in which Anglo-American music for many decades occupied a dominant position within what Regev describes

history of Soviet colonization of Poland and Anglo-American cultural imperialism? Through the lens of this album and his wider discography, the book will examine the various stages of migration, from experiences abroad, to return and circular migration. It will also discuss *Jarmark* (*Fair*) within the context of social remittances, that is, the impact that migrants have on stayers, both from afar and when they return.

This chapter introduces the context of this book by providing an overview of the history of Polish hip hop, and by extension, Eastern European hip hop. I discuss the career impact of rapping in non-English language in global music markets dominated by large Anglophone corporations. The chapter also explores linguistic aspects of Polish hip hop, including its blend of Polish and English and ties to Polish literary traditions.

The predicament of Polish rap

Academic discussions on Polish rap tend to begin with what it is not. It's not a genre pertaining to race, compared to its American counterpart (Kurnicki 2014: 148; Bandosz 2022: 22), nor is it a political genre, associated with either the left or the right (Kurnicki 2014: 162). It's also not a subculture with its own definitive set of values (Wójtowicz 2014: 188). And yet,

---

as 'pop-rock' (Regev 2002). In particular, in Eastern Europe, Anglo-American music was generally valued higher than music originating from countries such as Germany or Belgium. There was also a tacit recognition that rock music in countries such as Poland and Hungary was of a higher quality than Russian rock, and Estonian pop acted as an ersatz of western music in the rest of the Soviet Union (Ventsel 2016).

despite this, more recently Polish rap finds itself within the context of Poland's nationalistic turn (Majewski, Piotr. 2018). At the same time, several emerging Polish rappers are not white and rap about this racial difference. This shift is testament to the changing character of Polish rap and Polish society at large since the EU enlargement in 2004 after which Poland became a more multi-ethnic society. But, before discussing these shifts in Chapter 1, I want to give an overview of Polish rap's history and describe what is unique or particular to Polish rap, as well as what isn't.

Hip hop entered Poland in the 1980s when recordings of American rappers began to arrive, and musicians from the country's punk scene began to incorporate rapping, sampling and scratching into their music (Szarecki 2019: 155). However, it wasn't until the 1990s that Polish hip hop truly took shape. As Poland transitioned from communism to capitalism in the 1990s, socio-economic upheaval marginalized certain segments of society, particularly youth from housing estates (*blokowisko*), former state farm labourers and rural peasants, who bore the brunt of the changes (Pasternak-Mazur 2009: 9). The hip hop that emerged from these communities followed in the footsteps of gangsta rap, with its themes of drugs, crime and despair. The emergence of Polish hip hop coincided with the 'Golden Age' of hip hop, and gangsta rap's portrayal of inequality struck a chord with Polish rappers (Miszczynski and Tomaszewski 2017: 150). Themes from the punk scene of the 1970s and 1980s also shaped the Polish sound, characterized by a pessimistic outlook that advocated resistance against the system and a disregard for politicians (Kleyff 2014: 11). The first breakthrough artist in Polish hip hop was Liroy, whose rise to fame drew criticism from mainstream media (Szarecki 2019: 156). His commercial success also sparked condemnation from within the scene, culminating in 'Anty', a track by Nagły Atak Spawacza featuring fellow rapper Peja, which marked a significant moment in Polish hip hop history (Szarecki 2019: 156) as the first so-called 'diss' track.

Initially, Polish rap, particularly *uliczny* hip hop (street hip hop), struggled to gain popularity due to the prevailing optimism accompanying the transition to capitalism. It also clashed with the light-hearted and cheerful 'disco polo' music that dominated at the time (Pasternak-Mazur 2009: 9). As a result, it was an underground rather than popular music genre, which was exacerbated by the fact that it was associated with criminality. All this changed in the late 1990s. Disillusionment with capitalism, economic slowdown and soaring unemployment rates, peaking at nearly 20 per cent at the turn of the century, altered the social landscape (Pasternak-Mazur 2009: 9). Tackling themes of social inequality, violence, corruption and police brutality, rappers began to resonate with audiences, particularly recent graduates who were struggling to establish themselves amidst the economic recession (Pasternak-Mazur 2009: 9–10). A new generation of rappers came of age. Hemp Gru, Molesta, Pezet, Warszafski Deszcz (with Tede), WWO, ZIP Skład, DJ 600 V, along with Slums Attack, Nagły Atak Spawacza, and Gural – these rappers didn't just come from families affected negatively by the post-1989 economic changes; many of their parents actually benefited from the new economic order and political shifts (Majewski 2018: 5).

As such, Polish hip hop diverged from its gangsta rap roots and began to embrace local producers, the Polish language and domestic social issues. This shift stemmed from concerns about Polish rap being perceived as an inferior imitation of American music, despite its origins in genuine admiration and emulation (Szarecki 2019: 159). Critics lauded this evolution as 'intelligent hip hop', highlighting groups and artists like Paktofonika, Eldo (with his group Grammatik), Fisz and O.S.T.R. as prominent figures within this subgenre. This period also witnessed the professionalization of the hip hop scene, with dedicated rap magazines, websites and radio stations all beginning to appear. Every major city started to put on its own regular hip hop events, like Mega Club in Katowice, Słowianin in Szczecin, Eskulap in Poznań and Rotunda in Kraków (Kleyff 2014: 16). Then, in 1997, the first official Polish hip hop compilation album was released, featuring Warsaw artists such as Molesta and Trzyha, *Smak B.E.A.T. Records* (*A Taste of B.E.A.T. Records*) (Kleyff 2014: 16). From the late 1990s and through the 2000s, Polish rappers began to tour abroad, playing for the Polish diaspora in countries like the United Kingdom and Ireland, and in turn, foreign rap acts began to tour in Poland, attracting thousands of people (Kleyff 2014: 17). Other Polish artists caught on to rap's growing popularity and collaborated with Polish hip hop acts. Muniek Staszczyk from rock band T.Love collaborated with the hip hop group Zipera, Tomasz Lipiński from rock band Tilt worked with Warsaw rappers Vienio and Pele, the metal band Sweet Noise played with Peja and the Polish pop/R&B artist Natalia Kukulska collaborated with Tede (Kleyff 2014: 18).

With the rise in popularity of Polish hip hop came its commercialization. In the early 2000s, a new subgenre emerged known as 'hip-hopolo' which shunned politics and was more concerned with partying, romance and luxury brands (Pasternak-Mazur 2009: 16). Its emergence is commonly credited to the label UMC Records and its artists – such as 18L, Ascetoholix, 52 Dębiec, Owal and Mezo – who got the attention and support of major record companies and mainstream media outlets due to the perceived lack of taboo subject matter in their songs (Kleyff 2014: 18). Derided by hardcore hip hop fans as selling out, hip-hopolo artists were largely responding to the decline in sales resulting from the rise in MP3s and illegal internet downloads. While hip-hopolo enjoyed some popularity, the subgenre faded, and Polish hip hop proper retreated underground as radio stations and TV stopped playing rap and festivals stopped booking hip hop acts.

As the 2008 financial crisis hit the Polish economy, the underground hip hop scene had an unlikely resurgence. Rappers started sharing their material for free on the internet and began to use nascent social media platforms like MySpace, Facebook and YouTube. Independent rap labels were formed, and rappers started their own clothing brands to make up for the lack of profits from music (Kleyff 2014: 19). All this activity resulted in somewhat of a rebirth of Polish hip hop in the 2010s. Former Polish hip hop heavyweights such as Molesta, Warszafski Deszcz, Mor W.A. and Kaliber 44 returned to the scene while rap also started to find favour again in popular culture: rappers began to appear on both the small and big screens and became ambassadors for all sorts of different brands (Kleyff 2014: 20). But Polish media and big record labels still continued to ignore the genre until 2012 when the hip hop film *Jesteś Bogiem* (*You Are God*, dir. Leszek Dawid) was released and made Polish hip hop impossible to ignore. Thereafter, Polish rappers got their own shows, both on commercial and public radio stations, while the media began inviting them to comment on pop-cultural events (Kleyff 2014: 21).

Since Poland's accession to the EU, Polish rap has also found increased popularity abroad. Mass migration to countries such as the United Kingdom created new audiences for so-called 'heritage act' Polish rappers that were in high demand among the post-accession diaspora. This phenomenon has also given rise to new sub-scenes of first-generation or mixed-heritage Polish rappers, such as the UK Polish grime scene, creating music that bridges both Polish and host country cultures (Rymajdo 2016; Rymajdo 2019). But, much like other types of Polish music, with the exception of classical, jazz (Mazierska 2019; Rymajdo 2019) and metal, Polish rap has found little commercial or critical interest abroad, outside of Polish diaspora communities. There are also few Polish rappers who have extensively collaborated with artists from the West.

The development of Polish hip hop shares similarities with other Eastern European countries, where American hip hop gained popularity in the late 1980s, coinciding with the collapse of socialist regimes. This led to the widespread distribution of illegally copied cassettes and CDs at bazaars, shaping postsocialist aesthetics and people's relationships with Western music. Much like in Poland, generations growing up in former Soviet Bloc nations experienced first-hand the chaos of postsocialist transition, facing violence, corruption, poverty and instability. Hip hop emerged as a means for individuals to express their experiences and find strength to overcome these challenges, particularly for young men facing high unemployment. Additionally, throughout Eastern Europe, hip hop was viewed as a symbol of status due to its association with US popular culture. People who embraced hip hop saw themselves as cosmopolitan, capable of engaging with Western cultural products, which were typically costly to produce and consume (Miszczynski and Helbig 2017: 6).

As Eastern European hip hop developed and shifted into the mainstream, it also faced stigma for being 'inauthentic' due to its perceived disconnect from hip hop's African American roots and Black identity. However, each country's post-socialist relationship with the United States has influenced how each scene flourished in its own unique ways. Different levels of access to US music and the varying states of local economies following the collapse of the Soviet Union have led to an abundance of scenes that are linked both to their US origins while being inexorably tied to each country's domestic reality. For example, in Albania, hip hop has played a significant role in politics, providing a platform for alternative political identities and expressions. Macedonia's hip hop serves as a platform to express ethnic and cultural differences, acting as a cultural mediator to bridge ethnic divides (Miszczynski and Helbig 2017: 4). Russian rap, drawing parallels with Russia's literary tradition, serves as a dissenting voice questioning power in a country with suppressed freedom of speech

(Miszczynski and Helbig 2017: 4). Interestingly, in Serbia, the hip hop community was initially made up of mostly middle-class youth emphasizing cosmopolitan identities, but by the late 1990s, it embraced diverse subcultures, including *dizelaši* associated with street crime, helping hip hop in Serbia move beyond top-down, middle-class morals. Hip hop's association with emerging postsocialist class identities is also evident in Slovak rap, characterized by a masculine narrative of capitalism promoting upward social mobility and conspicuous consumption. Capitalist mobility is also present in Estonian rap, framed within rhetoric emphasizing modernization and globalization (Miszczynski and Helbig 2017: 5).

The textual and musical qualities of Polish rap

Musically, Polish rap has a lot in common with the conventions of American rap, in that it's the result of combining two forms of art: rhythmically spoken words, a beat, and samples (Mastalski 2014: 108). Like bricolage, the first Polish hip hop artists 'cut' and 'glued' together fragments of other people's compositions (both from classical and popular music genres), combining them with fragments of adverts or politicians' speeches, seemingly to say: 'I'm taking a piece of this culture where I am excluded, repressed and marginalised' (Mastalski 2014: 112). Also, much like in the case of American rap, Polish rappers' flow could take a simple rhyme and imbue it with expressive fluctuation (Mastalski 2014: 110). Hip hop scholar

Arkadiusz Mastalski points to 'Dalej' ('Next') by Miuosh as a classic example.

Similarly to its Afro-American predecessor, Polish rap also evolved with the traditions of battle rap (Deditius 2014) and beefs (Krakowski 2014). How to redefine the concept of 'keepin' it real' within the Polish context became a leading topic (Krakowski 2014: 64) of conflicts between rappers, as did the issue of representing (Krakowski 2014: 75). Political scientist Krzysztof Krakowski argues that three ideological conflicts emerged: unambiguous rap versus rap posing intellectual challenges (Krakowski 2014: 76); gangsta rap versus rap that brings people together (Krakowski 2014: 77); and commercial rap versus underground rap (Krakowski 2014: 79), while linguist Sabina Deditius describes Polish battle rap as intertextual, interweaving motifs referring to Polish culture, and frequently featuring insults with a complex syntactic structure, as well as successful parodies of other people's songs (2014: 55).

While scholars acknowledge Polish battle rap's American roots, they also point to its Polish ones. Two narratives emerged. The first is the aforementioned *uliczny* hip hop, springing from the *blokersi*, that is, frustrated young men, who came of age during Poland's transition to capitalism (Szarecki 2019: 156). The other 'involves the reception of hip hop through the works of nineteenth-century poets, in particular those who became pivotal to the formation of national consciousness, positioning rappers as heirs to the Polish literary tradition' (Szarecki 2019: 156). Polish rappers such as Ryszard 'Peja' Andrzejewski and Dominik 'Doniu' Grabowski have described Adam Mickiewicz as the 'original Polish rapper', underlining Mickiewicz's ability to write rhymes and write them quickly (Aniskiewicz 2021).

Warsaw freestyler Proceentle also namechecked Mickiewicz, describing his 1840 Christmas Day battle of words with fellow Romantic poet Juliusz Słowacki as the original battle rap (Deditius 2014: 39). The Polish rap band Kaliber 44 went even further by naming themselves after a line in the Mickiewicz poem *Forefathers' Eve* (*Dziady*) where Mickiewicz proclaims that the saviour of Poland will be someone whose name is 'forty and four'. Their debut album *Księga tajemnicza: Prolog* (*The Mysterious Book: Prologue*) continues the Mickiewicz references by reflecting the drama's romantic and spiritual elements: 'the music's dark tones, the rappers' calls for mystical inspiration, and Catholic symbolism recall the themes, settings, and plot of Mickiewicz's piece' (Bandosz 2022: 23). By doing so, Kaliber 44 'set a precedent for future artists, some of whom misinterpreted Kaliber 44's experimentation with Polish Romanticism as a renewal of a pure, national identity' (Bandosz 2022: 24).

When it comes to language, at first, Polish rappers wouldn't attempt mixing Polish with other languages in their lyrics, aside from peppering their songs with a few English swear words. An anomaly was the 1997 released song 'Your Face' by the hip hop group Thinkadelic which featured the Polish American duo P'Am singing in English. But as more Poles became proficient in English, more hip hop songs that incorporated English began to appear. New school rappers like Żabson and Schafter are especially known for their English-peppered lyrics. Żabson imbues his texts with words like 'vibe', 'slime', 'hype' and 'flex' used by American trap artists, while Schafter adds English words and phrases as a sonically pleasing addition, or to create lines that rhyme

(Szufladowicz 2020). Still, when the rapper Bedoes released the English-language EP *2119* as an addition to the deluxe version of his 2019 *Opowieści z Doliny Smoków* (*Tales from the Valley of Dragons*) it was only a nice curiosity. It failed to make any mark outside the borders of Poland and neither did it become a fan-favourite like many other releases from Bedoes' Polish-language discography (Kempiński 2023).

1 Poland's postsocialist history and the rise of Taco Hemingway

In this chapter, I'll discuss Poland's postsocialist history, using Taco Hemingway's rise as a case study to illustrate wider changes. For example, I'll point to differences between classical Polish rappers and Hemingway's generation; while the former were mostly working-class youth, Hemingway and his contemporaries were middle class and well educated. This will illustrate how Poland has changed over the past thirty years, arguably becoming wealthier and more cosmopolitan. I'll explore how Polish hip hop has both rebelled against the new reality (as in the case of the early rappers) and reflected it (as in the case of the latter). Additionally, I'll describe Poland's populist turn and identify rap's role within it. Finally, I'll situate the book theoretically, adding to discourse on European hip hop within the context of postcolonialism and migration.

A short overview of Poland's postsocialist history

In 1989, Poland's Iron Curtain came down. Its transformation from communism to democracy began in Gdansk shipyard when the trade union Solidarity (Solidarność) grew into a broad anti-authoritarian social movement, which gained the support of millions of Poles. The end of state socialism and the introduction of market capitalism changed the lives of Poles immensely. Most importantly, the rule that the state must ensure full employment of its citizens was abolished. Another change was the privatization of state assets. Finally, Poles got easier access to credit. These changes, initially seen positively as injecting dynamism into the moribund economy of the late-socialist period, in due course proved to be a crude instrument of social stratification (Mazierska 2022: 276).

In 1990, Poland held its first pluralist elections since 1947, with Solidarity leader Lech Wałęsa assuming the presidency and fellow Solidarity member Tadeusz Mazowiecki becoming prime minister. This marked the beginning of wide-ranging economic reforms aimed at transitioning Poland rapidly towards a market economy (Lukowski and Zawadzki 2019: 410). These reforms, often referred to as 'shock treatment', effectively curbed skyrocketing inflation and facilitated favourable renegotiations of the country's substantial foreign debts, with additional financial assistance from Western institutions. However, the immediate consequence of this shock treatment was a sharp rise in unemployment, significantly impacting a large segment of the Polish population, who suddenly found themselves without jobs. The restructuring of heavy industries like coal mining posed particular challenges, and other sectors also experienced significant setbacks. Regions such as Łódź and the Northwest (Mazury), reliant on single major employers, particularly in industries with predominantly female workforces like textiles, were hit hardest. Manual labourers, especially those formerly employed in state farms, also faced declines in real wages and social status. Additionally, despite increased emphasis on education and professional qualifications among the younger generation, fewer people from rural backgrounds pursued higher education. Agriculture remained a notably underdeveloped sector, with its low yields and smallholdings (Lukowski and Zawadzki 2019: 418). As such, by the 1990s, between 10 and 20 per cent of people were unemployed (Mazierska 2022: 276) as factories shut and the welfare state was rolled back. As a result, poverty again became prevalent in many parts of Poland.

The negative changes were felt the more acutely, as they were unexpected and were regarded unjust. After all, the Solidarity movement was supposed to represent workers. To a large extent, it was also a reaction to declining living standards in the second half of the 1970s and the perception that the *nomenklatura* (the higher echelons of the Party) was lining their pockets at the workers' expense. The fall of state socialism was meant to halt and quickly reverse these negative phenomena. Instead, in the 1990s, it deepened them. This situation fuelled frustration, anger and nostalgia for 'communism'. It also led to a belief that Poland is not a good country for 'ordinary Poles' – moving abroad was a better option. Hence, the period after 1989 saw an increase in migration, which gained momentum when Poland joined the EU in 2004.

Nonetheless, following 1994, real incomes experienced growth alongside the influx of foreign investment. By 1998, inflation had dropped to less than 10 per cent, ensuring currency stability. During the period spanning from 1993 to 1999, the per capita gross national product (GNP) of the Polish population surged from 33 per cent to nearly 40 per cent of the European Union average. By the early 2000s, private enterprises contributed to over two-thirds of Poland's GNP (Lukowski and Zawadzki 2019: 418). However, economic prosperity and development became increasingly concentrated in the capital region, leaving smaller cities and rural areas behind or even witnessing regression, which led to depopulation. One significant contributing factor was the deteriorating infrastructure, exemplified by the reduction of rail and bus routes. Disparities between the East and West of the country became more pronounced, exacerbating historic urban/rural, big city/small city, and East/West divides.

The first decade or so after the fall of the Iron Curtain was dominated not only by technocratic-liberal solutions, such as those of Finance Minister Leszek Balcerowicz but also by the idea that these are the *only* solutions. If some people did not like them, it was the problem of the said people, not the government. This was expressed by Balcerowicz's haughty disdain for the 'naive belief . . . that things can be explained to people'.

The new reality was reflected in Polish hip hop as rappers wrote about the social inequality that resulted from transformation. In this way, somewhat ironically, Polish hip hop came across as more Polish than the country's other music genres (Pawlak 2004: 39). The Polish hip hop of this era was also very much focused on friendship and nationalism, counselling that you can only rely on your 'ziomek', that is, brethren (countrymen). It reflected a generation whose parents were either neglectful because of social problems like alcoholism caused by the economic downturn or simply too overworked to give much time to their children (Kleyff 2014: 10–11). Feelings of hopelessness and a sense of being betrayed by the global capitalism, which had entered Poland, also found its reflection in Polish hip hop's focus on locality. Polish rappers, so-called 'local patriots' (Pawlak 2004: 42), wrote rhymes that focused on their own city, their own town, even their own village, block, street and bench, with this hyperfocus on their own turf becoming somewhat of a shield and a resistance against the forces of globalization (Pawlak 2004: 40). This focus on one's own surroundings meant that the Polish hip hop sound also diverged, as local dialects found their way into rappers' texts and the style of music referred to the current inspirations of people from a given city. For example, Warsaw was very much into the dirty sound of New York, while Poznań was like the American West Coast, inspired by Californian G-funk (Kleyff 2014: 15).

Two quintessential Polish hip hop films also capture this inward-focused mentality especially well. The first is *Blokersi* (dir. Sylwester Latkowski), a 2001 documentary about Polish hip hop artists and the problems of Poland's youth, and the second is the aforementioned *Jesteś Bogiem* (*You Are God*, dir. Leszek Dawid), a 2012 biographical film that charts the beginnings of Katowice hailing hip hop group Paktofonika as they struggle with the clash between art and consumerism at the turn of the century. While *Blokersi* depicts how Polish hip hopers such as Peja from Slums Attack and Eldo from Grammatik grew up, found friendship and made music hanging out outside blocks of flats in their respective localities, *Jesteś Bogiem* (*You Are God*) depicted how Paktofonika made their first and only album *Kinematografia* (the group's Piotr 'Magik' Łuszcz killed himself just after they completed making the record), knuckling down in the small confines of each other's apartments to record the tracks. By often showing the members of Paktofonika walking through the city listening to music through their headphones, it also communicated that for this particular generation, hip hop was literally a sonic protective shield from the hostile outside world (Jamrozik 2016: 218).

While the opposition to the technocratic neoliberal solutions that increased Poland's GDP, but also brought a high level of inequality and marginalization of the Polish province, was initially fragmented, it gained in force and coherence in the 2000s, both on the right and on the left. The opposition from the left was eventually incorporated into the technocratic liberal centre, while the opposition on the right solidified, leading to the creation of the 'Law and Justice party (Prawo i Sprawiedliwość)' in 2001. This party, effectively led by the Kaczyński brothers who used to be close allies of Lech Wałęsa, adopted a governing style emphasizing moral renewal, concern for ordinary citizens and opposition to perceived elites. One of their principal ideas was a belief in the role of the state as an instrument of economic redistribution, chiefly through generous child support whose ostensible goal was to halt the country's declining birth rate. While its success on this account was at best modest, as part of a coalition government with Self Defence (Samoobrona Rzeczpospolitej Polskiej) and the League of Polish Families (Liga Polskich Rodzin), Law and Justice succeeded in transforming the economic situation of millions of Polish families on low and middle incomes. The resulting high growth rates, reduced unemployment and increased employment practically eliminated poverty in Poland.

Internal conflicts led to the collapse of the coalition in 2007, with Law and Justice emerging as an unpredictable party, prone to extreme actions, and unable to form stable alliances. As such, while the 2007 parliamentary election campaign unfolded against a backdrop of economic prosperity, sociopolitical tensions were high, fuelled also by conflicts between Law and Justice and its main opposition party, Civic Platform (Platforma Obywatelska). Civic Platform's extensive programme titled 'Poland Deserves an Economic Miracle' (Polska zasługuje na cud gospodarczy) focused on modernization and infrastructure development, emphasizing a liberal economic model. Key elements included reducing social spending, recognizing the family as a primary provider of care, and introducing competition in social services. In contrast, Law and Justice's programme 'We Care for Poland. We Care for Poles.' (Dbamy o Polskę. Dbamy o Polaków.) continued the party's conservative approach from 2005, addressing citizen-friendly governance, support for entrepreneurship and state subsidiarity. Civic Platform won.

The subsequent 2011 election saw shifts in party ideologies. Civic Platform moved away from its liberal ideas, abandoning flat tax and public service commercialization. Their second term introduced controversial reforms, including changes to the pension system and lowering the mandatory education age. A scandal involving politicians eating octopus in luxury restaurants further tarnished the party's image, depicting it as detached from ordinary people (Gabryszak 2019: 103). Not surprisingly, 2015 saw Civic Platform adjust its election message, placing greater emphasis on social democracy and public services development. Law and Justice's policy programme centred around a PLN 500 family allowance, proposals to extend parental leave and raise income thresholds for family benefits, and lowering the retirement age.

Law and Justice also focused on theories construed around 'gender' and nation, with 'gender' and specifically the LGBT community characterized as an 'ideology', while nationalism was reflected in the belief that Poland is a sovereign country. They advocated that the decisions of Polish bodies, most importantly those of the parliament and government, should overrule those of pan-national institutions, such as the European Union, which Law and Justice and its allies portrayed as Germany-dominated. This stance also resulted in criticism of the 'open borders' attitude exercised in Germany under Angela Merkel during the migration crisis in 2015.

The focus on preserving Poland and Polishness as a cohesive cultural identity, based on Christian traditions, led also to the tightening of the abortion law. While most likely the supporters of Law and Justice did not identify with all ideas and policies of the party, there was enough in this 'package' to ensure its comprehensive victory in the 2015 parliamentary elections, to the disappointment of Polish neoliberal elites, which saw it as a victory of bigotry and narrow-mindedness.

This development is arguably not surprising given that the institution of the Roman Catholic Church and its attendant values are deep-rooted in Poland and the relatively high religiousness of Poles continues to stand out in Europe (Perdał 2022: 77). Some of this devotion dates back to the conceptualization of Poland as 'the Christ of nations', the Christian defender safeguarding the Eastern borders against incursions by non-believers. A messianic doctrine from the New Testament based on the principles of brotherly esteem and regard for one another, it first became widespread in Poland through the activities of the Reformed Churches in the sixteenth and eighteenth centuries. It was then adopted by Polish Romantics who likened the partitions of Poland to the Crucifixion, the national spirit akin to an immortal soul, and the resurrection serving as a promise for the future resurgence of the Polish nation.

The USSR's stringent stance on religion and decades-long attempts to diminish the church's significance in Poland perpetuated the tradition of resistance. The Catholic Church emerged as a leading force in the neoconservative counter-revolution to communism (Nowak 202: 227), aided by the election of Karol Wojtyła to pope in 1979. It was then strengthened when the initially left-wing Solidarity workers' movement was taken over by a right-wing narrative approved of by its Western allies, most notably America's President Reagan. Indeed, by 1991, the bulk of Solidarity had fragmented into several rival trade union organizations and a host of populist anti-communist and nationalist-Catholic groupings (Lukowski and Zawadzki 2019: 412).

When the Iron Curtain fell, the high status of the Catholic Church was evident in various ways, such as by the swift introduction of religious education into all state schools by the inaugural government led by Tadeusz Mazowiecki. This significant shift unfolded without the scrutiny of parliamentary debate, as the overwhelming Catholic majority seemed to preclude the need for such discussions. The church's influence extended beyond education too, as evidenced by the controversial 1993 abortion ban. Despite impassioned street protests, vigils and parliamentary debates, Poland adopted one of the world's most restrictive abortion laws, allowing only three exceptions. The death of John Paul II in 2005 triggered another surge of devotion while the church's close alignment with Law and Justice meant its lobbying for even stricter abortion laws came to fruition in 2020, when the law changed to only permit abortion to safeguard the life or health of the woman or where a pregnancy results from rape or incest.[1]

With the ascent of Law and Justice and their emphasis on nationalism, it's perhaps unsurprising that during the early 2000s, Polish rap began to serve as a tool for shaping a pop-nationalist narrative to (re)construct Polish collective memory (Majewski 2018: 6). For instance, the National Center for Culture (NCK) commissioned Peja to rap an excerpt from Adam Mickiewicz's national epic, *Pan Tadeusz* (*Master Thaddeus*) (Szarecki 2019: 161). Over time, such institutions began to sponsor rap songs that portrayed a specific interpretation of the national past, with the patriotic theme gaining considerable popularity. Hits like 'Patriota' (Patriot) by Zipera and 'Kochana Polsko' (Dear Poland) by O.S.T.R. exemplify this trend. Rappers also displayed their patriotism through gestures such as wearing the colours of the Polish flag or through self-identifying narratives like 'I, a Pole', contrasting

---

[1] However, in some respects, the church is losing its grip on Polish society. In 2019 revelations presented in an investigative documentary titled *Tylko nie mów nikomu* (*Tell No One*, dir. Tomasz Sekielski) delved into child sexual abuse perpetrated by Polish priests. The documentary exposed the active role played by the church in concealing the abuse, especially the highest echelons of the Catholic hierarchy. The church took an aggressive stance, portraying itself as the true victims of a witch-hunt orchestrated by the media. This defensive strategy proved to be counterproductive – according to the church's own data, in 2021, only 28.3 per cent of the population attended Sunday mass, a staggering drop from 47.6 per cent in 1991 (Orliński 2023).

themselves with 'them', that is, government officials or pro-European and pro-market elites (Pasternak-Mazur 2009: 13). In this way, hip hop provided a platform for voicing various fears and anxieties associated with regime transition and Poland's integration into the EU.

Over time, this genre, known as 'patriotic rap', began to receive backing from right-wing political parties, their affiliated media outlets, nationalist organizations, the Catholic Church and a growing number of state and local government institutions typically aligned with promoting nationalist sentiments (Majewski 2018: 7). With Law and Justice assuming power in 2015, rap also found a place in state-owned media.

Taco Hemingway and the millennial generation

Taco Hemingway, real name Filip Szcześniak, was born in 1990 in Cairo, Egypt. His father worked for an import/export firm, moving the family to Guangzhou, China, when Hemingway was two. In 1996, the Szcześniaks moved to Warsaw. In a 2015 interview with news website Gazeta.pl, Hemingway revealed that growing up, he spoke English with his mother and sister and Polish with his father, who played a part in his developing passion for rap (Nazaruk 2015). His parents divorced in 2004.

Hemingway studied cultural studies at the University of Warsaw. In 2012, he began studying for a master's degree in anthropology at University College London. While in London, he began posting rap songs on YouTube, using the alias Foodvillain. Rapping in English on illegally downloaded

British-American rapper MF DOOM's beats, he recorded his first mixtape *Who Killed JFK* in 2011. In 2013, he adopted the pseudonym Taco Hemingway, which was his alias on a FIFA football game, and one he described as not being inspired by the writer Ernest Hemingway, but rather, a name he thought sounded good (Nazaruk 2015). The same year, Hemingway released his first English-language EP titled *Young Hems* via Bandcamp. Both releases garnered little interest.

When he came back to Warsaw, Hemingway got a job in advertising, but abandoned it in favour of becoming an English translator. In the meantime, he was writing his second EP, the Polish-language *Trójkąt warszawski* (*Warsaw triangle*). On 19 December 2014, the release was made available as a free digital stream on YouTube and as a free download on the rapper's website. A day after the premiere of the EP, Hemingway played his first gig at Warsaw's Kulturalna, a cafe and music venue situated in the Palace of Culture and Science.

Trójkąt warszawski (*Warsaw triangle*) received favourable reviews from critics. For example, journalist Dawid Bartkowski gave the album a rating of 3/5, praising the descriptions of Warsaw and of the protagonists' lives (Bartkowski 2014). What he liked less was Hemingway's voice, which although he noted suited the album's structure and plot, was somewhat monotonous. In turn, the music portal Uniwersum Dźwięku noted the album's sharp observations and original wordplay, as well as praising its producer Rumak (Maciej Ruszecki) for use of samples from old films (Uniwersum Dźwięku 2014).

The success of *Trójkąt warszawski* (*Warsaw triangle*) led to Hemingway signing with the hip hop label Asfalt Records, with whom he released his next project, 2015's *Umowa o dzieło* (*Contract work*). In 2016, Hemingway's third Polish language EP, *Wosk* (*Wax*), and his first studio album, *Marmur* (*Marble*), were released. In 2017, his fifth EP, *Szprycer* (*Spritzer*), became a commercial success, selling 30,000 copies. In April 2018, Hemingway collaborated with Polish rapper Quebonafide in recording and releasing the album *Soma 0,5 mg*, which went platinum. He released LP *Café Belga* and EP *Flagey* the same year. In 2020, he released two LPs within one week of each other, first *Jarmark* (*Fair*), then *Europa* (*Europe*). Although not as commercially successful as some of his previous works, the albums still did well. *Jarmark* (*Fair*) was the eighth best-selling album in Poland in 2020, while *Europa* (*Europe*) took ninth place. Hemingway released his latest LP *1-800-Oświecenie (1–800-Enlightenment)* in 2023. In total, he has sold over 400,000 albums in Poland, making him one of the country's best-selling Polish rappers. At the time of writing in February 2024, he had 2,239,560 monthly listeners on Spotify (Spotify 2024).

Much of Hemingway's output has met with critical acclaim. He's been nominated for a Fryderyk award (the Polish equivalent to a Grammy) thirteen times, winning for his albums *Umowa o dzieło* (*Contract work*), *Marmur* (*Marble*), *Szprycer* (*Spritzer*) and his collaborative album *Soma 0,5 mg* as part of the duo Taconafide with Quebonafide. He won in the 'Song of the Year' category for *Jarmark* (*Fair*)'s 'Polskie Tango' (Polish Tango). The only artist to win the award three times in a row, he's also the only rapper nominated and awarded in the Song of the Year category. In 2018, alongside Quebonafide, he was nominated for an MTV Europe Music Award for Best Polish Artist.

In 2019, Hemingway announced a concert at Warsaw's PGE Narodowy stadium alongside the popular singer-songwriter and Polish X Factor winner Dawid Podsiadło. Tickets sold out in three hours and the arena was filled with 73,000 fans, with the artists selling more tickets than American heavy metal band Metallica and British rock group Coldplay. Also in 2019, he was ranked tenth on the list of 'Most Influential Poles' by weekly news publication *Wprost*. As of 2018, Hemingway is believed to live in London with his girlfriend Iga Lis (Baliński and Strowski 2019).

Often collaborating with schoolfriend Rumak on the music for his releases, Hemingway started his career rapping over simple beats and samples. Many of his earlier releases lacked melody as he delivered his raps in a monotonous flow where the most emotion he could muster was sounding exhausted, irritated or, at times, surprised. His debut album *Marmur* (*Marble*) was especially lacking in melodies and choruses, with minimalist production from Rumak. As he progressed in his career, Hemingway began experimenting more, incorporating elements of trap, electronic music and pop, into his productions. He also began working with different producers, such as the Holland-born Borucci, who said in an interview that Kanye West, Timbaland and The Neptunes were his inspirations (Szufladowicz 2020a). With Hemingway expanding his musical horizons, especially from *Szprycer* (*Spritzer*) onwards, when the rapper also began using Auto-Tune, critics noted that he had the potential to be a crossover artist (Stackiewicz 2016). Features such as frequent collaboration with Artur Rojek, former guitarist and lead singer of the Polish alternative rock group Myslovitz, have also pushed Hemingway into new musical territory. However, it's for his lyricism, which is often structured around a single overarching narrative, that Hemingway has received the most praise.

Hemingway broke onto the scene with a distinctly preppy look, with neatly shorn 'short-back-and-sides' hair that he's only intermittently deviated from to grow it out into a ponytail. This stands in contrast to many of the rappers who came before him, who styled themselves after gangsta rappers, and many of his contemporaries, who, heavily tattooed with brightly coloured hair, bring to mind Soundcloud or mumble rappers. Hemingway's face, predominantly clean-shaven aside for his distinctive moustache, also brings to mind millennial hipsters, rather than anything typical of either Polish or Western rappers.

Also atypically for artists of his calibre, Hemingway has largely shunned making music videos to his songs. The videos that do accompany some of his biggest tracks don't feature Hemingway himself, being either animated or made up of a collage of photos and found footage, as in the video for 'Polskie Tango' (Polish Tango) from *Jarmark* (*Fair*). Hemingway is also a predominantly introverted stage performer. Often wearing a baseball cap, he raps his songs with little interaction with the audience. It's a manner that seems to adjust a little when he performs with other artists, as part of Taconafide with Quebonafide, for example, or with Dawid Podsiadło, when he seems more animated and looks like he's enjoying himself. In contrast to other Polish rappers who tour countries with large Polish diasporas, Hemingway has also almost exclusively performed live in Poland. An exception is a 2018 gig in London. Fan footage posted on YouTube shows the gig was well attended (Cebula 2018), with Hemingway speaking to the audience in Polish.

Given his look, it's perhaps not surprising that Hemingway is a Polish millennial, or a member of what scholars describe as the 'open-borders generation'. Unlike those born in the late 1950s in Poland, who've been called the 'crisis generation' because for them the experience of stark economic crisis, the birth of the Solidarity movement and martial law in 1981–3 was formative (Sadowski and Mach 2021: 4) and those born in the early 1970s, who came of age during the political breakthrough of 1989, with the hopes and risks inscribed in the systemic change itself, the 'open-borders generation' began adulthood at the time of Poland's accession to the European Union and entrance to the Schengen Area (Sadowski and Mach 2021: 4). Differing to the previous cohorts, their entire life has been lived in a democracy and a market economy, and they have no memory of communist times, with western Europe as an important reference point (Sadowski and Mach 2021: 8).

In many ways, the structure of opportunity changed favourably for Hemingway's generation. Higher education became much more accessible, for example. As such, while there is continuity of Polish hip hop's previous incarnations within Taco Hemingway's output, not least the fact that his music can be described as 'intelligent hip hop', Taco Hemingway and his successors such as Mata represent a new turn in the genre with a distinct, unashamedly middle-class voice. On the other hand, among this generation, there is a widespread sense of insecurity and instability, especially when they're compared with previous generations (Sadowski and Mach, 2021: 4). While the 'transition generation's first job would often be a permanent contract, only 18 per cent of the 'open-borders generation' found that this was the case for them (Sadowski and Mach, 2021: 12). This is consistent with wider trends: younger cohorts in Europe were considered to be facing a relatively less stable work situation than their predecessors and are sometimes called the 'precarious generation' or the 'jilted generation'. However, in Poland, the prevalence of temporary employment is higher than the EU average for 15–39-year-olds (Sadowski and Mach, 2021: 13).

Hemingway's early releases, 2014's *Trójkąt warszawski* (*Warsaw triangle*) and 2015's *Umowa o dzieło* (*Contract work*), are especially exemplary of Polish millennials as the generation whose lives are characterized by instability, especially within the realm of work. For example, on autobiographical tracks like '100km/h' Hemingway laments that being a rapper is no way to earn enough of a living to start a family. Similarly, on 'Awizo' (Advice) he details how he spent half of his wages on trendy foods like hummus, halloumi and kale, in this way suggesting that his earnings don't total to very much. His protagonists don't fare better: on *Umowa o dzieło* (*Contract work*)'s '+4822', a young man shows off with 100 and 200 *zloty* bills, but in actuality has no money given that his only form of work is an unpaid internship.

Scholars write that pronounced differences in the type of first work contract among the different cohorts went along with the expansion of the market economy in Poland. The majority of Poles born in 1988–9 acquired their first job and most subsequent work experiences in private companies (Sadowski and Mach 2021: 14). This has resulted in the 'open-borders generation' becoming less egalitarian as 'the reality of functioning within a private company, with a clearly established, uneven distribution of profit between the entitled owners and the employees, makes young Poles prone to accepting larger income discrepancies in the whole of society' (Sadowski and Mach 2021: 20). As such, for the time being, the generation born in 1989 doesn't appear inclined to challenge the prevailing economic system. This stands in stark contrast to, for instance, American millennials who formed the nucleus of the Occupy Wall Street movement (Sadowski and Mach 2021: 20).

A lack of egalitarianism and, in general, political interests is reflected in the things Hemingway writes about millennials being concerned with. For example, *Trójkąt warszawski* (*Warsaw triangle*) details the lives of three young Varsovians: the protagonist, his ex-girlfriend and her new love interest Piotr as they make their way through Warsaw's bars and nightclubs. For example, on 'Marsz, marsz' (March, march), Hemingway's protagonist describes how he and his fellow Varsovians drink heavily and take drugs, while on 'Wszystko jedno' (Doesn't matter) he details their casual sex encounters. That Polish millennials are more accepting of the inequalities of society is evidenced by the fact that Hemingway and his protagonists are more often than not accepting of their lot, as when Hemingway describes how on the one hand he has no money, but on the other, he finds some kind of comfort in the situation: 'I could avoid spending cash, but I prefer to despair' ('Mógłbym mniej wydawać forsy, ale płakać wolę').

Not surprisingly, Hemingway has been very popular with Polish millennials, tapping into and reflecting so accurately many aspects of their lives. Interestingly, Hemingway has also been singled out by scholars as a rapper whose oeuvre holds a mirror up to this generation (Kołodziejczak and Smoter 2018) as one who is materialistic, ambivalent and constantly searching for new experiences.

Trójkąt warszawski (*Warsaw triangle*)'s success arguably lies in the fact that Hemingway's criticisms of millennials are covert: for example, on 'Szlugi i kalafiory' (Fags and cauliflowers) he raps: 'A city of concrete and lost phones. I walk along a path strewn with glass from mobile phones' ('Miasto betonu i pogubionych telefonów. Idę ścieżką usłaną szklanym szronem'), and some of his biggest barbs are directed at the main protagonist, that is, himself, like when he describes how the album's hero is always on the search for the newest spots and the trendiest handouts: 'I was here, I was there, but who wasn't?' ('Jestem tu, byłem tam, zresztą w sumie kto nie był'). The great attention Hemingway pays to listing specific nightclubs and particular streets, such as the shot bar Przekąski Zakąski, the bar/club Plan B or the street Kredytowa (on which another trendy bar is located: Miłość), imbues the album with cultural capital that only millennials (and younger generations like Gen Z) will be privy to. In this way, Hemingway singles them out as the listeners who he not only most aligns with but also most values. It creates the sense that while Hemingway is criticizing millennials' specific qualities – the need to be adored, whether in romantic relationships or on social media, their fickleness – in consumption patterns and in sexual relationships, and their slavish devotion to Western products and brands – he's also extolling their knowledge and taste, ultimately sympathetic to their plight as a generation focused on individualism. He achieves this through an ambivalence in the lyrics, by providing the listener with multiple perspectives of the same situations: there isn't a wrong or a right, only different points of view. In this way, Hemingway signals that every millennial and their specific worldview is worthy of respect. And, as the references to the times of People's Republic of Poland in the form of samples used suggest, Polish millennials are in some way the continuation of previous generations who too fell in love, went drinking and were unhappy. By doing this, Hemingway communicates that Polish millennials' shortcomings aren't entirely their fault, but a result of what went before, of how they were raised.

That millennials make up a large proportion of Hemingway's audience, who number 4.1 million across music streaming and social media platforms like Spotify, YouTube, Instagram and TikTok (Soundcharts 2024), also makes sense in light of their sheer number being the result of the 1980s baby boom in Poland (Sadowski and Mach 2021: 8). In 2018, they made up 22.8 per cent of the population. Combined with Gen Z, who made up the biggest cohort with 23.4 per cent, Hemingway's core listeners come from the demographic representing half the current population of Poles (Sadowski 2018).

Migration within the work of Taco Hemingway

In the view of hip hop scholars of European rap, when it comes to hip hop in Europe, far from copying its American version, it too is a medium through which artists develop a voice in their own national and local contexts. Academics such as Griffith Rollefson argue that hip hop artists are the vanguards of a new generation that reframes what it means to be European in a global world and challenge what they describe as 'ahistorical notions of national belonging', responding to ever louder calls for tighter border controls with the postcolonial mantra: 'we are here because you were there' (Rollefson 2017: 2). As immigrants from former colonized countries settle in the heart of the ex-colonial capitals, hip hop helps them force their nation to see them as an inherent part of its identity. Elsewhere, scholars describe the transnational character of European rap, born from the movement of people between countries and interaction between different diasporas, rather than musicians' attachment to a specific place (Solomon 2009). I will now attempt to demonstrate where Hemingway's work sits within this wider landscape.

Migration from Poland

Poland has a long history of migration, with all strata of society leaving across different times in history. From royals to soldiers, missionaries and artists, and also common people such as farmers, merchants, traders and craftsmen, people left for good reason. War, hunger, epidemics and persecution, all drove people to leave, as did a desire to improve living standards, though scholars usually group Polish migrants into two categories: political and economic (Davies 1981: 275; Davies 1984: 193). The Industrial Revolution and its accompanying demographic explosion was also the precursor to mass migration, as work had to be sought further and further from home. Destinations such as Germany, France and North and South America proved viable for many Poles. However, migration was not always permanent, especially for those who left family and property behind. Indeed, mass labour migration came to a halt with the outbreak of the First World War. In turn, the Second World War was a period of compulsory mass migration, when Polish citizens were taken from German-occupied areas for forced labour in the Reich to the USSR (Davies 1981: 286).

Many notable literary, artistic, scientific and political figures were migrants: Adam Mickiewicz spent five years exiled in central Russia, after being active in the struggle to win independence for his home region, which had been partitioned by Russia in the late eighteenth century. He spent most of the rest of his life in France, where he created his most famous works. Juliusz Słowacki, who alongside Adam Mickiewicz and Zygmunt Krasiński is considered one of the 'Three Bards' of Polish Romantic literature, also left Poland after the defeat of the November 1830 Uprising, settling in Paris. It was also the reason that Joachim Lelewel, author of 'For our freedom and yours' (one of the unofficial mottos of Poland, originating from a banner commemorating the Decembrist revolt), left Poland.

The Great Emigration, as the emigration of thousands of Poles, especially from the political and cultural elites after the failure of the November Uprising, came to be known, has had a great impact on Polish identity and culture. The idea that both individual and national freedom must be achieved was particularly forcefully expressed in the works of Polish Romantic writers in exile, who continue to be celebrated, taught on school curricula and referenced by artists across the board. For example, Polish cinema continues the Romantic tradition, with tragic hero protagonists who fail but fight on, such as the soldier Maciek in Andrzej Wajda's *Popiół i diament* (*Ashes and Diamonds*). Polish musicians too reference the Great Emigration. For example, Czesław Niemen, one of the most important Polish singer-songwriters and rock balladeers of the twentieth century, pays homage to Juliusz Słowacki and poet Cyprian Norwid, who also left during the Great Emigration, on albums such as his 1978 *Idée Fixe*, released with his band Aerolit.

Other prominent emigres include composer Fryderyk Chopin, physicist Marie Skłodowska-Curie and novelist Joseph Conrad (Józef Konrad Korzeniowski). Many intellectuals also left during the Second World War (Dziewanowski 1977: 244) and over 2 million highly educated Poles left in the 1980s. Because of these emigration waves, there has come to be 'a tradition of elite exile that makes it easy to understand framings of the post-2004 wave of highly educated Poles to the United Kingdom and Ireland as a tragic brain drain' (White et al. 2018: 17). On the other hand, Poland's accession to the European Union in 2004 made migration a more positive and less permanent strategy for many who left, opening doors to better work, at lower personal cost, and to combining work and travel for adventure (White et al. 2018: 18). It attracted both migrants from larger cities, and those from more rural areas where unemployment was high. As a result, in many European countries such as the United Kingdom, Norway and Iceland,

Poles became the dominant ethnic minority population. Here, and elsewhere in the European Union, circular and temporary economic migration predominated. Economist Marek Okólski (2001) coined the term 'incomplete migration' for migrants who earned a living abroad but 'lived' in Poland, where their families remained and to which they frequently returned (Okólski, quoted in White et al. 2018: 17). As a result, 'Many migrants, feeling that they had feet in two countries, began to acquire a sense of dual belonging' (White et al. 2018: 19). This identity is further complicated by the fact that some Poles emigrate to different places throughout their lifetime.

Circular migration and the failure of the 'Grand Narrative'

While Polish migration has a long history, scholars argue that representations of migrations have been petrified in the periods of the Cold War and the transformation between 1989 and 2004 (Galasińska and Horolets 2012: 128). They assert that it was in these two periods that cultural meanings of migration were negotiated in private and semi-public spheres and formed the 'Grand Narrative' of economic migration (2012: 128). Characterized by valour and success achieved abroad, this narrative has its roots in the defeat of the 1831 Uprising against the Russian Empire's occupation of Poland when a large wave of intelligentsia fled to France (Galasińska 2010: 940). Crucially, in its focus on what can be achieved, the narrative silences the question of how it can be achieved (Galasiński and Galasińska, quoted in Galasińska and Anna Horolets 2012: 128).

As such, during many years in communist Poland, it wasn't that important how one earned one's money as long as one earned it. Becoming rich, no matter how, was part and parcel of opposing the political system of communist 'equality' and rebelling against the authorities in a very personal way (2012: 128). Hegemonic narratives about the success of migration hid – or at least softened – the part of the narrative that dealt with undignified work and the poor living conditions of migrants in the receiving country (2012: 128).

Taco Hemingway's return to Poland and his first Polish EP can be likened to post-2004 migrants who are left out socially and economically in a way that migrants from southern European countries are not (Sabater 2015: 227). Experiencing 'the humiliation resulting from social and professional degradation' (Galasińska and Horolets 2012: 131), they are left with feelings of betrayal by the promise of the 'Grand Narrative' and shame at an inability to fulfil it for themselves. For example, *Trójkąt warszawski* (*Warsaw triangle*)'s main protagonist is a wandering loser in life and in love, as described on 'Marsz, marsz' (March, march), where Hemingway not only alludes to wandering via the song's title, but the track itself is about someone failing to get what they want. This seems a strong metaphor for a migrant who has failed to find what he was looking for in his destination country and, therefore, failed to fulfil the 'Grand Narrative'. Hemingway uses samples from documentaries and films that depict or describe people on the margins of society to hammer the point home: a snippet of dialogue from the 1957 documentary film *Paragraf Zero* (*Paragraph Zero*) by Włodzimierz Borowik detailing social pathologies, hooliganism and prostitution and dialogue from the 1970 film *'Konsul' i inni*

(*'Konsul' and others*, dir. Krzysztof Gradowski), which portrays the real-life swindler Czesław Śliwa.

In comparison, Piotr, the competitor in the love triangle of *Trójkąt warszawski* (*Warsaw triangle*), while criticized for his materialism, is still undeniably 'better off' than Hemingway's hero. He has both more disposable income, and he gets the girl. As such, Piotr can be read as a metaphor for the Poles who chose not to abandon their country and because of this have come out on top. This trope continues on the song '900729', where Hemingway also alludes to being behind his countrymen, complaining that while his friends are becoming businessmen, he hasn't yet achieved anything; while they're 'civilized', he's still 'wild'. He explains that their maturity is evident in how they dress and behave. For example, he lists how they've swapped their Vans trainers for leather boots, while noting the way they talk has also changed: in their new vocabulary, 'siki' (piss) has been replaced by 'mocz' (urine). He continues with this theme on 2016 released LP *Marmur* (*Marble*) where on the track 'Żywot' (Life), he describes that while his schoolfriend has settled down and has a child, he's still walking around with a quart of alcohol in his pocket. Similarly, on 'Świat jest WFem' (The world is like PE) he likens the Polish hip hop scene to a football team, where he is perennially the new teammate or the one on the bench – crucially, not on the same level as his peers.

The subject of a loser in love is also explored on *Umowa o dzieło* (*Contract work*). For example, on 'A mówiłem Ci' (I told you so), the protagonist picks up a girl only to be ditched for a man of better means (communicated via the rival's expensive Armani suit and the Japanese alcohol, sake, that he's drinking).

He's also a loser in other ways. On opening track 'Od zera' (From zero), Hemingway reveals his hero is a precarious worker, as also underlined by the EP's title. But the track's title also suggests having to start from scratch, again communicating that those who have left Poland and return must start from the beginning. The album's sonic lack of progression from *Trójkąt warszawski* (*Warsaw triangle*) makes a similar point. It's as if Hemingway is stuck in the 'beginner' phase of his career, and either scared or unable to progress. That this pervasive sense of failure and a 'back to the start' mentality is the result of a failed migration is suggested as the protagonist reveals he's just returned from the United Kingdom, where he had spent a year: 'I breathe the Vistula River, earlier, it was a year by the River Thames' (Oddycham Wisłą. Wcześniej rok nad Tamizą), he raps on 'Od zera' (From zero). His precarious status is again underlined on '6 zer' (6 zeros), where he admits to accepting bank transfers from his mother and having to economize by switching beer brands from the foreign Grolsch to the Polish Łomża.

The failure of migrating to the United Kingdom is alluded to or discussed across several other tracks in Hemingway's discography. For example, *Marmur* (*Marble*)'s title can be read as a nod to migrant Polish Romantic poet Cyprian Norwid, who wrote the poem 'Marmur – biały' (White Marble), a love letter to Greece, but who lived an impoverished life in Paris. Hemingway namechecks Norwid again on *Europa* (*Europe*) track 'Luxembourg', comparing himself to the poet (as well as Norbi, a 1990s Polish hip-hopolo artist) with the lyrics,'Pół Norbi, pół Norwid' (Half Norbi, half Norwid). The theme continues on *Marmur* (*Marble*)'s 'Żywot' (Life), that is, Hemingway's life story. Here, the rapper recollects moving to London, where he found his studies unsatisfactory and the city hostile, while also admitting that his friends have deemed his English-language music, recorded with borrowed money, as inferior to his Polish texts. On *Europa* (*Europe*) Hemingway also discusses living in London with little means, for example, referencing the yellow label 'reduced' stickers at supermarkets on his track 'Sztylet' (Dagger).

Meanwhile, *Marmur* (*Marble*)'s focus on the duality of the protagonist, characterized as both, two sides to Hemingway, but also as two different characters within the plot of the album, can be likened to the 'incomplete migrants' who work in one place but live in another (White et al. 2018: 17). Here, the Hemingway we have gotten to know over the course of the previous releases meets his alter ego, that is, his ambition. Characterized as crass and greedy, he can be read as the next incarnation of the kind of Pole Hemingway has described to us before, as in the character of Piotr from *Trójkąt warszawski* (*Warsaw triangle*). While lacking the kind of qualities Hemingway holds dear – intellectualism over materialism, for example – this alter ego is nevertheless seemingly more successful than the Hemingway protagonist we have gotten to know, suggesting that those who stay in Poland have more ambition, drive and ultimately success.

Disappointing return

Writing about migration to and from Poland since EU accession, scholars Anne White et al. write that there wasn't a big wave of Poles permanently returning after 1989. Some tried coming back but didn't stay, feeling that their real home was in the foreign country where they'd migrated to (2018: 20). Hemingway's later work fits this description of a migrant, as he keeps trying to leave Poland after his initial return, both physically and emotionally. For example, one of the themes of *Marmur* (*Marble*) is a rejection of the current reality of Poland and a longing for the past, which brings to mind post-war migrants who practise 'restorative nostalgia', that is, attempt a transhistorical reconstruction of a lost home (Boym 2001: 41). This is illustrated by tracks such as 'Żyrandol' (Chandelier), where Hemingway is much more at home among the archaic architecture of the hotel than the modern shops outside. References, such as the line 'Moje oczy i ten miszmasz są jak Pawlak i Kargul' (My eyes and this mishmash are like Pawlak and Kargul), a nod to PRL-era film *Sami swoi* (*Our Folks*, 1967) by Sylwester Chęciński continue the longing for a long-gone Poland. It's also evident in the album's overall narrative, focused as it is on pulling Hemingway out of his current reality, signalled via the hotel porter banning him from using his mobile phone. In turn, on 'Deszcz na betonie' (Rain on concrete), he admits that life has changed since he started rapping in Polish, but adds that now is the time to leave, and he will see his listener, metaphorically, on his next record. The sentiment finds its echo in the video for the song, whose animation is a series of stills, with the camera moving across them, conveying a sense of motion. Motion is also conveyed more straightforwardly: we see the protagonist travelling on a train, as he returns from the seaside to Warsaw.

The theme of being disillusioned with and attempting to escape continues on 2018's *Café Belga*. On the opening track of the same name, Hemingway compares himself to Polish emigrant writer Witold Gombrowicz, who was a staunch anti-nationalist and criticized class roles in Polish society and culture. Scholar Benjamin Bandosz (2022) asserts that Hemingway aligns himself with Gombrowicz by self-reflexively critiquing Polish hip hop's masculinity and patriotism, mirroring Gombrowicz's critical engagement with Polish Romanticism's cultural legacy, which led to Polish identity being associated with the partitions and struggle against foreign oppressors (Bandosz 2022: 25). Bandosz also asserts that '*Café Belga* exemplifies an (im)maturation in the style of Gombrowicz by adopting his playful and irreverent attitude toward truth, fiction, and identity' (Bandosz 2022: 33). Citing an interview which bookends the tracks, where the interviewer ponders whether he is talking to the 'real' Taco Hemingway, that is, Filip Szcześniak, or his persona as a rapper, Bandosz asserts that Hemingway 'signals his intention to experiment through the artificiality of his rap persona and to reconfigure his relationship to Polish hip hop' (Bandosz 2022: 33).

I would argue that this at times confusing duality can also be likened to post-2004 migrants, who, thanks to 'transnational practices' such as phoning, video calling and frequent visits, often feel that they're in both their migration country and Poland, at the same time (White et al. 2018: 19). The feeling of being in between two places is even articulated by Hemingway seemingly journeying through time, as on the track '2031', where the rapper imagines himself past his prime, after reaching the peak of his career in the year 2021. The track ends with Hemingway ruminating on his future son receiving royalties from albums which became popular again after his death, only to wake up from this 'dream' back in 2018. Visually, this is a theme that can also be gleaned from the few music videos that Hemingway has featured in, notably with Quebonafide. With sets for songs 'Tamagotchi' and 'Kryptowaluty' (Cryptocurrencies) made to look like the 1980s and 1990s, they give the impression of time travel.

Hemingway continues some of the same themes of isolation, depression and disillusionment with fame on *Flagey*, a bonus EP released alongside *Café Belga*, which takes its name from Place Eugène Flagey, a square in Brussels where Café Belga is located. On 'Pokédex', he once again says he refuses to turn up to accept 'stupid awards' and emphasizes that he sees himself as a writer first and a rapper second. He also states that he doesn't want to associate with other hip hop artists and mentions the possibility of retiring by the end of the year, hoping to be remembered as a legend like American rapper Nas and British rapper Skepta. He also expresses dissatisfaction with his career, rapping about not wanting fans or fame and simply wanting to escape to Asia with his girlfriend.

On 2020's *Europa* (*Europe*), Hemingway continues his 'escape' journey, using a diary style to place the protagonist driving through Europe. The album is more critical of Poland and Hemingway's life there. He returns to the theme of being chased by paparazzi on tracks like 'Sztylet' (Dagger) and 'Ortalion' (Nylon), reacting with aggression not seen before. For example, on 'Sztylet' (Dagger), he raps about wanting to assault a paparazzi photographer: 'Nie mam już siły, Kiedy zobaczę tego paparazzi, to będę go bił' (I've run out of patience, the next time I see the paparazzi, I'm beating him up). On 'Ortalion' (Nylon), he finds happiness as a tourist with his girlfriend, enjoying anonymity in Europe. But this album also shows his dissatisfaction with being a rapper. He talks about wanting to be 'something more' on 'Na Paryskie Getto Pada Deszcz' (It's Raining on a Paris Ghetto), saying he'd rather be a writer than a rapper. Finally, the disappointment is also communicated by the fact that Hemingway's output can be characterized as depicting victimhood, which stands in contrast to the 'winning' mentality of gangsta rap, which is characterized by braggadocio lyrics and excess. Hemingway, even on tracks that he made after achieving great success, doesn't paint himself as a winner in any way.

Whether this is the 'real' Hemingway is debatable. In his 1996 book *Performing Rites: On the Value of Popular Music* sociomusicologist Simon Frith contends that popular music artists not only perform their music but also construct carefully curated personas that embody particular identities and attitudes. Frith examines how artists navigate between different personas and genres, emphasizing that the construction of a musical persona is a deliberate act of performance that shapes both the artist's public image and the reception of their music, arguing that these personas are integral to how audiences perceive authenticity and meaning in popular music.

Philip Auslander builds upon Frith's insights by delving deeper into the performative aspects of musical personas and their intersections with broader cultural and social contexts. In his books such as *Music in the Twentieth Century* and *Performing Glam Rock: Gender and Theatricality in Popular Music* Auslander draws on performance theory to analyse how musical performances are structured as cultural acts. He extends Frith's analysis by exploring how performers in genres like glam rock use theatrical elements to challenge conventions and blur the boundaries between music, theatre and visual art (Auslander 2004, 2006). Auslander's analysis emphasizes the role of visual representation and media technologies in shaping and disseminating musical personas, highlighting how these personas are not static but dynamic constructs that evolve through interactions with audiences and cultural discourses.

Hemingway effectively stopped giving interviews once he became successful, but even if he did, interviews can still be part of an artist's armoury in creating their musical persona, according to Frith and Auslander. As such, it's impossible to know whether the image of a frustrated rapper who sees himself as a loser of the 'Grand Narrative' is a true reflection of Hemingway's perception of himself or the persona he keeps evolving through subsequent records. However, its consistency throughout his output can at least be interpreted as a comment on the failure of the 'Grand Narrative' of Polish migration. Crucially, it comes across as authentic. Indeed, I would argue that the ongoing, almost relentless, preoccupation with the negative aspects of his career, such as being recognized and followed by paparazzi, as well as boredom with his own artistry, suggests a real feeling of disappointment at not having made it as a rapper in the United Kingdom, where potentially his career might have played out differently. This is underscored by the fact that more recently Hemingway has expressed this even more explicitly than before. On a guest verse on Mata's 2021 'Kurtz' from the album *Młody Matczak* (*Young Matczak*) Hemingway bitterly declares that when he was Mata's age he wanted to be a world-famous musician, recounting trying to make it in the United Kingdom and failing. He admits that the experience broke his heart and made him question pursuing this lifepath. That Hemingway would have preferred to have made it in the United Kingdom (and in this way have had a chance to become a global artist as someone who raps in English) is supported by the fact that the rappers he feels an affinity for, or would like to be like, are internationally renowned British, American and Canadian ones: his tracks make reference to artists such as Biggie Smalls, Tupac Shakur, MF DOOM, Nas, Skepta, Kendrick Lamar and Drake. On 'Kurtz', he even compares himself to Kanye West, decrying that at Hemingway's then age of thirty-two West had already written his critically acclaimed *My Beautiful Dark Twisted Fantasy*.

While making it as an English-speaking rapper seems an ever more unlikely possibility, as the name of Hemingway's 2022 tour *Pocztówka z Polski Tour* (*Postcard from Poland Tour*) suggests, Hemingway might have at least achieved his mission of escaping Poland – it implies he has left Poland for good, via the insinuation he is a tourist, writing postcards from places he is now just visiting, rather than living in.

2 The textual analysis of *Jarmark*

At the beginning of 2020, Hemingway was about to go on his sixth tour to celebrate his successful LP *POCZTÓWKA Z WWA, LATO '19 (POSTCARD FROM WWA, SUMMER '19)*, which was nominated for a Fryderyk award and was the tenth highest-selling album in Poland the previous year. However, due to the outbreak of COVID-19 in February that year, the tour was postponed. Soon after, Hemingway teased that he might be releasing new music on a '#hot16challenge' campaign to promote fundraising for medical personnel. On 25 June 2020, a photo of the rapper working on new music started making rounds on the internet. On 3 July, he made a guest appearance on Artur Rojek's single 'A miało być jak we śnie' (It was supposed to be like a dream). Later that month, together with the group PRO8L3M, Hemingway founded a music publishing company called 2020. On 10 July, two days before the presidential runoff between Law and Justice incumbent Andrzej Duda and centrist candidate, the Warsaw mayor Rafał Trzaskowski, Hemingway dropped the single 'Polskie Tango' (Polish Tango), with its accompanying video released on YouTube. The single broke the daily streaming record on Spotify Poland, previously held by Hemingway's 'W PIĄTKI LEŻĘ W WANNIE' (ON FRIDAYS I LIE IN THE BATH), gaining over 560,000 plays. On YouTube, he garnered over 2.5 million views in 24 hours, also breaking his previous record.

On 28 July, Hemingway announced via Instagram that the release of his upcoming albums *Jarmark* (*Fair*) and *Europa* (*Europe*) had been postponed. A day later, the lead single from *Europa* (*Europe*) 'Michael Essien Birthday Party' (Michael Essien's Birthday Party) came out on Hemingway's birthday, with the album release dates confirmed for 4 September 2020. *Jarmark* (*Fair*) came early, with the rapper making it available on streaming services and as a free download on his website on 28 August. Released via Hemingway's publishing company Taco Corp and 2020, on 4 September both albums' physical versions went on sale.

Writing about the album on Instagram, Hemingway described *Jarmark* (*Fair*) as his first release since *Trójkąt warszawski* (*Warsaw triangle*) where he wasn't rapping about his 'current situation', and told his followers that they'd find storytelling, a handful of childhood memories and social observations within the twelve songs. He revealed, too, that the process of making the album had been an intensive one, where he spent a lot of time writing and refining the songs, thinking about each topic carefully.

The album was produced by multiple producers, including Hemingway's longtime collaborator Rumak (Maciej Ruszecki), who produced the tracks 'Łańcuch I: Kiosk' (Chain I: Kiosk), 'Łańcuch II: Korek' (Chain II: Traffic Jam), 'Łańcuch III: Korpo' (Chain III: Corpo), 'Nie Mam Czasu' (I Don't Have Time), 'Dwuzłotówki Dancing' (Two-Zloty Coins Dancing), 'Szczękościsk' (Lockjaw) and the bonus track 'Sznycel'

(Schnitzel). Lanek (Kamil Łanka), a rapper/producer known for working with Polish rappers Białas and Bedoes, produced the lead single 'Polskie Tango' (Polish Tango). The Holland-born Borucci (Boris Neijenhuis) produced 'Influenza' and 'POL Smoke'. Pejzaż, aka Bartosz Kruczyński, considered one of the most talented and versatile Polish producers (Grupa 2020), produced 'Panie, to Wyście!' (Sir, it's You!) and '1990s Utopia', while CatchUp (Grzegorz Szczerek), an emerging producer, rapper and TikToker, produced the track 'W.N.P.', i.e., 'Wychowała Nas Pornografia' (Pornography Raised Us).

Hemingway also enlisted various collaborators to sing and rap on the album, including Artur Rojek, who guest features on the 'Łańcuch' (Chain) trilogy, Katarzyna Kowalczyk, from the folk/electronic duo Coals, who sings on the track '1990s Utopia' and, Gruby Mielzky, who guests on the track 'Influenza'. The album also features the voice of well-known lector Tomasz Knapik, who reads lines in the 'Łańcuch' (Chain) trilogy.

In this chapter, I'll provide a focused textual analysis of a selection of songs on *Jarmark* (*Fair*), while providing an overview of the remainder. In doing so, I'll explore how the album reflects Poland's postsocialist history through its narrative tropes. I'll examine the changes that led to the country's populist turn. For example, I'll delve into *Jarmark* (*Fair*)'s political commentary, zooming in on tracks like 'Polskie Tango' (Polish Tango), which calls out the Law and Justice party for fear-mongering propaganda. I'll also discuss the trilogy of songs titled 'Łańcuch' (Chain), pointing to Poland's growing xenophobia towards immigrants, especially those from Ukraine. Finally, I'll analyse the powerful role of the Catholic Church in Poland, as presented by Hemingway.

I'll do so predominantly by analysing Hemingway's use of poetic devices. These devices, from repetition to metaphor, operate by infusing language with layers of meaning, creating vivid imagery, and evoking emotional responses in listeners. Repetition, for instance, involves the deliberate use of words, phrases or sounds to emphasize key elements of a text. In turn, metaphor functions by drawing unexpected connections between disparate elements, allowing the writer to convey abstract concepts through concrete imagery.

In the realm of hip hop, these poetic devices are commonplace. For example, in Nas' iconic track 'N.Y. State of Mind' metaphors like 'I never sleep, 'cause sleep is the cousin of death' paint a vivid picture of urban life, while an effective simile is Lauryn Hill's 'Me without a mic is like a beat without a snare' on The Fugees' 'How Many Mics'. In turn, repetition, as seen in Kanye West's 'Power' (No one man should have all that power), reinforces key themes. Moreover, hip hop artists utilize various other poetic devices like alliteration and assonance (the repetition of the same or similar vowel sounds within nearby words) to enhance the musicality of their lyrics, creating rhythm and cohesion within their verses.

Finally, I'll analyse *Jarmark (Fair)*'s music within the context of postcolonialism, highlighting how the album reflects Poland's cultural dynamics and aspirations. I'll describe how Jarmark (*Fair*)'s sound, heavily influenced by contemporary Western artists, signals Hemingway's desire for international recognition, while also serving as a subtle critique of Poland's populist movements.

'Polskie Tango' (Polish Tango)

That *Jarmark* (*Fair*) is an album about Poland's transition from communism to market democracy is signaled by its title, which is a reference to the Warsaw market Stadion Dziesięciolecia (10th-Anniversary Stadium), a stadium opened in 1955 which under the Polish People's Republic was a venue for party and state festivities. After the fall of the Iron Curtain, it became a bazaar called Jarmark Europa, becoming one of the most overt symbols of capitalist Poland. (That this is the market that Hemingway alludes to is also confirmed by the title of *Jarmark* (*Fair*)'s sister record, *Europa* (*Europe*)). There are also plenty of other references to demonstrate such a reading. For example, samples from Polska Kronika Filmowa (The Polish Film Chronicle), a 10-minute-long newsreel that was shown in Polish cinemas between 1944 and 1995 and presented current events, cultural commentary and opinion journalism, are used to show how Poles reacted to the post-transition changes and imbue the album with a certain realism.

Hemingway also references the transition more directly, acting as a narrator giving his listeners a history lesson. In doing so, he tries to explain why Poland has ended up where it has. He begins his lesson with the lead single 'Polskie Tango' (Polish Tango) whose story starts in the 1990s, when Poland was at the beginning of its transition from socialism to market democracy. It's also when the 'EU effect' began to manifest via domestic reforms in response to the anticipated expectations of the European Union that led to various concessions and the impression that Poland had to give up some of its identity. Hemingway is referring to this time with the opening line of the song: 'W latach 90tych nie miałaś tożsamości, Zachód pędził do przodu, zachód nie miał litości' (In the 90s you had no identity, The West rushed ahead, the West had no mercy).

In turn, the recurring metaphor of the 'tango' encapsulates the experience of navigating Polish identity amidst sociopolitical turbulence by referencing the complex dance of the tango, which can be said to symbolize the struggle inherent in Polish life during transition. The title also references the 1964 play *Tango* by Polish dramatist Sławomir Mrożek, which revolves around a dysfunctional family that symbolizes a society undergoing disintegration. The head of the family, Stomil, represents the avant-garde artist who declares the decline of traditional values and societal norms. His son, Artur, is the protagonist who seeks to rebel against his father's chaotic and liberal ideology. Mrożek uses absurdity to highlight the contradictions and crises within human relationships and societal structures. Taco Hemingway's 'Polskie Tango' (Polish Tango), through its reflection of the rapid modernization and westernization of Poland during the 1990s, highlights a similar sense of contradiction and crisis. Mrożek's *Tango* ends with a tango dance, which can be read as symbolizing mainstream culture, suggesting those 'values' won. Hemingway similarly seems to be suggesting that mainstream culture in his context, that is, capitalism, won out in Poland. Like in many previous songs where he points out the absurdity and dangers of the new capitalist Polish way of life, in 'Polskie Tango' (Polish Tango) he too underlines its resultant image-obsessed masculinity, where 'gym bros' drink fortified yoghurt drinks with 'well-balanced protein'.

Hemingway also uses contrast as a tool to illustrate the tension between Poland's postsocialist past and capitalist present. This is evident in lines like 'Mówi się: "szare bloki"? Gdzie, kurwa, szare bloki?, Tutaj wszystko pstrokate – baby, typy i yorki' (They say: 'grey blocks'? Where the fuck are the grey blocks? Here everything is colourful – women, guys, and Yorkies [Yorkshire Terriers]). Here, the contrast between the expected greyness and the actual garishness of contemporary life highlights confusion and cultural dissonance. In turn, Hemingway utilizes imagery to ground the narrative in a specific sociohistorical context. Descriptions like 'plastikowe zabawki' (plastic toys) and 'fajne nowe pornoski' (cool new pornography) vividly capture the consumerist explosion of the 1990s, highlighting both the allure and superficiality of material wealth.

Repetition, a powerful device in hip hop often used to create a hypnotic rhythm and reinforce key messages, is also a key tool in Hemingway's armoury on 'Polskie Tango' (Polish Tango), where he employs it both lyrically and thematically to underscore the cyclical nature of the struggles and paradoxes inherent in Polish identity and society. First, the lines 'Tańczę polskie tango, Nogi w błocie mam, bo Wisła to grząskie bagno' (I dance the Polish tango, My feet are in the mud, because the Vistula is a treacherous swamp) are repeated verbatim in the chorus, anchoring the song with a consistent and memorable motif.

Another notable instance of repetition is found in the line 'I to ma sens, sens, sens, sens, sens . . . ' (And it makes sense, sense, sense, sense, sense . . .). The accumulation of the word reflects a sense of frustration and resignation, as if the narrator is trying to convince themselves of the sense behind their experiences but ultimately revealing a deep-seated uncertainty. This repetition creates a rhythmic insistence that mirrors the internal conflict and the difficulty of finding clarity and purpose.

In terms of thematic repetition, the song's core theme is the contrast between 'old' and 'new' Poland. The rhetorical question 'Szare bloki? Gdzie, kurwa, szare bloki?' (Grey blocks? Where the fuck are the grey blocks?) is exemplary of Hemingway's depiction of the stark transformation of urban landscapes from the drab uniformity of communist-era housing to the colourful, consumerist reality of modern Poland, highlighting the sense of displacement and the struggle to reconcile these two eras.

The use of rhyme provides a rhythmic quality that enhances the song's flow. For instance, in the first verse, the rhyme scheme is consistent, with lines ending in 'tożsamości', 'litości', 'pościg' and 'głodni'. This creates a cohesive and melodic structure that draws listeners in and underscores the points Hemingway is making. In turn, the aggressive delivery of the raps – a departure from Hemingway's previous output – communicates a loss of patience. The beat too is aggressive and the tempo fast, with more detail to the production than Hemingway is known for – particularly effective are the muffled screams in the chorus and sirens in the second verse.

Sarcasm also serves as a tool for critique in 'Polskie Tango' (Polish Tango), like the address of contemporary conspiracy theories which mocks the irrational fears surrounding vaccines and technology, critiquing societal susceptibility to misinformation. Another example is when Hemingway subverts a poem by Władysław Bełza, written to preserve Polish patriotism during the country's partitions, replacing a reference to the White Eagle symbol of Poland with a line about white powder, that is, amphetamines, which Poland is known to be a big producer of (Reuters 2014). Other lines from the poem are also subverted to show the deterioration of Poland, such as a description of Poland as a fatherland fought for with blood and scars, to one characterized as a sandcastle won by a propaganda of fear. This line especially seems to be a direct criticism of Law and Justice, given that their campaigns had been described by critics as based on fearmongering, especially about the country's LGBT community, which Law and Justice had described as an ideology out to destroy Poland's family values rooted in the teachings of the Catholic Church.

The dialogic nature of Hemingway's subversion of Bełza's poem, where one line poses a question while the next one answers it, gives the impression of appraisal by the outsider, Hemingway, who seems to be putting Poland and Poles 'on trial'. This seems to be an indirect criticism of Law and Justice, as it criticizes the Poles who live in Law and Justice's Poland by pointing out their shortcomings. (Hemingway seems to foretell criticism he might receive for being a critical outsider on the song 'Panie, to Wyście!' (Sir, it's You!), where in another dialogic exchange a voice tells him to leave Poland, to which he responds that he can't because 'I'm from here'. Notably, he doesn't say that he 'lives here', which, perhaps unintentionally, underlines his position as an outsider.)

Hemingway also uses poetic invocation[1] to evoke emotional responses and provoke thought, adding layers of meaning to his social commentary. One prominent instance is the line 'Kto ty jesteś? Polak mały' (Who are you? A little Pole). He also evokes cultural symbols to underscore his critique. For example, the reference to Santa Claus, a symbol of consumerism and festive cheer, juxtaposed with Poland's national colours in the chorus, 'Narodowe barwy mamy jak Santa Claus' (We have national colours like Santa Claus), is used to suggest that national pride has become as commercialised and hollow as a commercial holiday.

Reference to the nation is also a recurring theme in the song. Phrases like 'Moim krajem może rządzić byle miernota' (My country can be ruled by any kind of mediocrity) and 'W moim kraju ta oświata to jest ciemnota' (In my country, education is ignorance) lament its current state. By referencing the nation, Hemingway personalized his critique, making it clear that his disappointment and frustration are deeply felt. This technique also aligns with hip hop's tradition of speaking truth to power and addressing the state directly in a confrontational manner.

In several parts of the song, Hemingway also indirectly invokes the audience, drawing them into his narrative and critique. For instance, in the line 'Proszę, by przestali, lecz się śmieją, mówią: "Dobra stary, ty no, kurwa, weź"' (I ask them to

---

[1] Poetic invocation refers to the use of direct address, often to abstract concepts, cultural symbols or entities, to imbue the lyrics with greater emotional and rhetorical power.

stop, but they laugh and say: 'You know what man, fuck off'), the conversational tone and direct speech draw the listener into the scene, making them a witness to the dialogue. This invocation of the audience serves to make the critique more immediate and relatable, as it invites listeners to see themselves in the narrative and consider their own positions.

The 'Łańcuch' (Chain) trilogy

The 'Łańcuch' (Chain) trilogy's premise is that Poland is made up of links in a chain, with the movement of each link having an effect on the next, and the whole. 'Łańcuch I: Kiosk' (Chain I: Kiosk) sets the scene with Hemingway showing how a mean-spirited action leads to another mean-spirited action, and how in this way, the victim becomes the mean-spirited aggressor themselves. Over a tension-building cinematic melody, Hemingway raps quickly, 'Oni są niemili, bo to . . . Ja jestem niemiły, bo to . . . Ty jesteś niemiła, bo to . . . łańcuch, Potem społeczeństwo jest niemiłe, bo to . . . łańcuch' (They're unpleasant because it's . . . I'm unpleasant because it's . . . You're unpleasant because it's . . . a chain, Then society is unpleasant because it's . . . a chain). It feels like a kind of modern-day hip hop interpretation of Karma.

'Łańcuch' (Chain) lays the blame for this domino effect on the world of work post-communism. Employing a narrative form and delivered by Hemingway in a serious, low-toned voice, 'Łańcuch I: Kiosk' (Chain I: Kiosk) sets the scene with a young man at a newsstand, a symbol of old economic practices persisting in the new market reality. The dilapidated state of the kiosk, covered in faded graffiti, mirrors the stagnant remnants of Poland's past within its current capitalist framework. The kioskarz (kiosk worker) embodies the disillusionment of the older generation, sceptical and tired of the new generation's demands.

Hemingway then shifts to the student's employment – working in a fast-food joint. His encounter with a demanding customer seems to underscore the menial and often demeaning nature of the jobs available to many young Poles. But the critique here is twofold: not only are jobs scarce and unfulfilling, there is also a lack of respect and understanding between different layers of society. The customer's insensitive inquiry about gluten in a bread roll also reflects a superficial and self-centred consumer culture that exacerbates this tension.

The mournful chorus, sung by Artur Rojek, underscores the pervasive bitterness and emotional numbing that result from these daily struggles. The lyrics 'Patrz mi w twarz, jest jak kamień' (Look at my face, it's like stone) and 'Nienawiść jest ślepa - tak już zostanie' (Hatred is blind – that's how it will remain) evoke a sense of enduring resentment and loss of empathy within society, suggesting that the hardships of the transition have hardened people. That Rojek already sang about hatefulness in his own song 'Nienawiść' (Hate) underlines the idea that when it comes to Poles, history keeps repeating itself and there seems to be no alternative. Rojek's defeated voice, which complements Hemingway's sombre tone, also seems to underline this hopelessness. It's a voice that seems to imbue what Polish writer and film director Tadeusz Konwicki has described satirically as 'the Polish Complex' in his eponymous 1982 novel, in which his characters lament the absurdity of their everyday struggles and mourn the fate of their country under communism, languishing in a state of inevitability and fatalism. In this way, Hemingway seems to be reiterating the point he was making in 'Polskie Tango' (Polish Tango) with his reference to *Tango* by Sławomir Mrożek – that Poles are trapped in cycles of fatalistic gloom, disheartened because of their history.

In the second part of the trilogy, 'Łańcuch II: Korek' (Chain II: Traffic Jam), over the same beat and melody, Hemingway highlights the xenophobic undercurrents that have surfaced in modern Poland. Rattled by the fast-food employee's spiteful quip that she should lose weight, the passenger of a Ukrainian immigrant's taxi verbally abuses the Uber driver. This encounter not only highlights the racial and ethnic tensions exacerbated by economic strain but also the scapegoating of immigrants for broader systemic issues. The Uber driver Dimitri's internal reflection on the 'udręka' (torment) of xenophobia emphasizes the emotional toll such prejudice takes on individuals, further illustrating the social fractures caused by economic upheaval.

In the final segment 'Łańcuch III: Korpo' (Chain III: Corpo), Hemingway focuses on Grzegorz, a corporate worker, and his moral and emotional conflict with the demands of his job. Tasked with laying off employees, Grzegorz embodies the human cost of corporate efficiency and profit maximization. The corporate environment is depicted as cold and exploitative, where even someone with a 'miły charakter' (nice character) is coerced into doing things he doesn't want to do.

Grzegorz's interaction with Antoni, an older employee being laid off, brings the narrative full circle. With the melody becoming more ominous in this version of the song, it's clear that a grim conclusion is coming. Antoni's subsequent employment at a kiosk, as revealed in the outro, symbolizes the cyclical nature of economic displacement and the persistence of precarious, low-status jobs despite promises of progress and prosperity. This return to the starting point of the narrative chain (łańcuch) suggests a stagnant, unchanging reality for many, where the old and the new economic systems fail to provide a dignified and stable livelihood. Indeed, through these interconnected stories and multiple character portrayals, Hemingway highlights how the new system of market democracy has failed to deliver its promises of better work and social harmony. Such a reading corresponds with recent reports which have found Poland consistently one of the countries with the longest working hours among European countries, coming only second to Greece in 2023 (Eurostat 2023).

As a sum of its parts, the 'Łańcuch' (Chain) trilogy is arguably one of the most effective parts of the album, much like American rapper Eminem's famous song 'Stan', which employs the cinematic technique of thrillers or horror movies where the audience knows more than the characters on screen (Fosbraey 2022: 57). Hemingway too structures the 'Łańcuch' (Chain) trilogy in such a way that we essentially know what's coming, not least because the beat and melody keep repeating too. It is worth evoking here a distinction between 'musematic' and 'discursive repetition', made by musicologist Richard Middleton. 'Musematic repetition' is an extended repetition of short musical units; 'discursive repetition' concerns longer units, at the level of the phrase (Middleton 2006: 17–18). The author links 'musematic repetition' with 'hypnotic' rhythmic patterns that can lead to a trance-like state in the audience, resulting in a collective loss of self (Middleton 2006: 19). In contrast, 'discursive repetition' is associated with a stronger engagement of the ego and the self (Middleton 2006: 20). While 'musematic repetition' captures immediate attention and creates memorable elements, 'discursive repetition' provides structure and helps in developing the song's narrative. In 'Łańcuch' (Chain), these two types of repetition work together to create an effective sense of dramatic irony, which enables listeners to be more invested in the story.

Moreover, several poetic devices are effectively utilized to enhance the narrative depth and lyrical impact. For example, Hemingway employs complex rhyme schemes to craft vivid and engaging narratives, as in the line 'Nagle przeklęta klientka zaczyna go nękać – czy w tej bułeczce jest gluten?' (Suddenly the darned customer begins to pester him – is there gluten in this bun?). Furthermore, throughout the trilogy, Hemingway employs metaphors and imagery to convey the themes of societal discontent and interpersonal strife. For instance, the description of the kiosk as a 'zgniło zielonkawy korpus' (decaying greenish body) in the first part conjures a visceral image of urban decay and desolation.

Hemingway also utilizes different forms of address to convey the interactions between characters and their societal contexts. For example, in the first part, the direct interaction between the student and the female customer asking if there's gluten in her bun brings immediacy and authenticity to the narrative. In addition to direct interactions, there are also instances of indirect address, as in the description of Dimitri's thoughts: 'Dimitri zostaje w korka środku myśląc sobie' (Dimitri stays in the middle of the traffic jam, thinking to himself), which allows listeners to empathize with their experiences on a deeper level.

Beyond individual interactions, the lyrics also address broader societal themes and constructs. For instance, the repeated refrain 'Oni są niemili, bo to . . . Ja jestem niemiły, bo to . . . Ty jesteś niemiła, bo to . . . łańcuch, Potem społeczeństwo jest niemiłe, bo to . . . łańcuch' (They're unpleasant because it's . . . I'm unpleasant because it's . . . You're unpleasant because it's . . . a chain, Then society is unpleasant because it's . . . a chain) reflects a collective addressing of societal norms and behaviours, inviting listeners to reflect on the systemic nature of negativity and its impact on social dynamics.

'Panie, to Wyście!' (Sir, it's You!)

In 'Panie, to Wyście!' (Sir, it's You!), Hemingway continues his depiction of hatred between Poles as resulting from the transition. Over a melancholic pop melody interrupted by aggressive interludes that resemble snippets from a conversation and Hemingway singing with Auto-Tune, a kiosk shop attendant is listed among people who hate their fellow Pole. Schoolteachers, employers, and internet trolls are also called out as being especially hateful: 'Nauczyciel cię nienawidzi . . . Pracodawca cię nienawidzi' (The teacher hates you . . . The employer hates you), with the repetition creating a rhythm of relentless animosity. In turn, the use of direct address ('cię', – you) makes the listener a direct participant in this hostile environment, enhancing the sense of universality of this experience.

Hemingway then uses a metaphor to describe the country as 'jedna wielka podstawówka' (one big elementary school), which suggests that Polish society is immature and characterized by pettiness, as if everyone is stuck in a perpetual state of childish conflict. The line 'Jej murów nie opuścisz nigdy' (You will never leave its walls) employs hyperbole to underscore the inescapability of this environment.

Sarcasm is a key device in the portrayal of societal norms and expectations. For example, the line 'Myślisz, że życie to więcej niż gotówka, że człowiek to więcej niż liczby (Bzdura)' (You think life is more than money, that a person is more than numbers (Nonsense)) juxtaposes genuine human values with the dismissive term 'bzdura' (nonsense). This highlights the disillusionment with a society that prioritizes materialism over humanistic values.

In the chorus, 'Robisz test DNA, żeby wiedzieć, gdzie jest twój dom, Biało-czerwona koperta, w środku wynik, że jesteś stąd' (You take a DNA test to know where your home is, a white-and-red envelope, inside the result: you're from here), Hemingway uses symbolism to critique the concept of national identity. The white-and-red envelope, symbolizing the Polish flag, contains a result that reaffirms the speaker's

Polish identity. However, the repeated refrain 'Sorry, nie mogę, bo jestem stąd' (Sorry, I can't, because I'm from here) juxtaposed with expletives such as 'wypierdalaj' (get the fuck out) suggests a bitter acceptance of an imposed identity, as if the speaker is trapped by their national identity despite societal rejection.

The second verse delves deeper into political criticism. The line 'Druga strona też nienawidzi' (The other side hates too) ephasises that hatred is not confined to one political faction but is a widespread phenomenon. Hemingway also highlights the disconnect between rural and urban populations by emphasizing class divides and the mutual disdain between different segments of society: 'Jesteś z małego miasta – elita się ciebie brzydzi' (You're from a small town – the elite despise you).

The chorus' repetition and the inclusion of aggressive commands like 'wypierdalaj' (get the fuck out) amplify the sense of hostility and rejection faced by individuals who critique the status quo. The culmination of this section with gunshots serves as a stark and jarring auditory metaphor for the violent silencing of dissent. In turn, the inclusion of the outro, a voiceover from a Polska Kronika Filmowa (Polish Film Chronicle) short about the opening of a McDonald's in Warsaw, is an ironic critique of the overblown importance given to Western consumer culture. It compares the arrival of McDonald's to significant national events, like bringing home the ashes of Polish pianist, composer and former prime minister Ignacy Jan Paderewski and the welcoming of American president George H. W. Bush.

'Dwuzłotówki Dancing' (Two-Zloty Coins Dancing)

On *Jarmark* (*Fair*) Hemingway both presents how the Catholic Church was inextricably tied up with Poland's transition and also criticizes its grip on Polish society. He does so predominantly on 'Dwuzłotówki Dancing' (Two-Zloty Coins Dancing), where over a minor key melody with dynamically delivered bars he describes what he sees as the Catholic Church's rampant capitalism.

The opening verse does much of the work of setting the ominous tone. Hemingway introduces the listener to a stark scene: 'Dusza przeklęta, pierwsza komunia święta, Gapią się na mnie trupy, z witrażu kostucha zerka' (Damned soul, first holy communion, Corpses are staring at me, the Grim Reaper is peeking from the stained glass). The juxtaposition of innocence ('pierwsza komunia święta' [first holy communion]) with morbidity (trupy [corpses] and kostucha [the Grim Reaper]) immediately connotes disillusionment as Hemingway's imagery evokes a sense of haunting and foreboding.

The narrative then transitions to a religious doubt, beginning with the line 'Kapłan kosztuje kawy i strasznie mnie, żłopiąc, beszta, Gada mi o szatanie i ważnych potworach z piekła' (The priest sips coffee and scolds me terribly, gulping, Talks to me about Satan and important monsters from hell). Hemingway's use of colloquial language ('żłopiąc' [gulping] and 'beszta' [scolds]) diminishes the priest's authority, rendering his warnings about damnation less credible. Hemingway further explores this topic with the line: 'Pan Jezus umarł dla mnie, a to nieprzeciętny gest, Choć nie wiem, czemu w wierze tyle kwestii sprzecznych jest' (Jesus died for me, and that's an extraordinary gesture, Though I don't know why there are so many contradictory issues in faith).

Much like the song's title, which alludes to the commercialization of religious practices and the transactional nature of faith, the song's chorus, 'Dwuzło- dwuzło- dwuzłotówki on me dancing' (Two- two- two-zloty coins on me dancing), uses repetition to emphasize the jingling sound of coins, a metaphor for the pervasive greed within the church. The message is strengthened by the fact that the chorus and melody of the song are a reference to 'Diamonds Dancing', a track by Canadian rapper Drake and American rapper Future, which details the excesses of the two artists.

The second verse continues the critique, highlighting the material excesses of the clergy: 'Proboszcz ciągle woził się w nowej furze, Pomyślałem: "bardzo lubi go ktoś na górze"' (The priest always rode in a new car, I thought: 'someone up there must really like him'). The metaphor of the 'new car' serves as a symbol of wealth and privilege, contrasting sharply with the church's message of humility and poverty. This hypocrisy is further emphasized through the repetition of the refrain, where the priest's 'cruisin' merolem' (cruising in a Mercedes) becomes a recurring image of clerical opulence. The use of the word 'memo' in the chorus also suggests that Hemingway is comparing the church to a capitalist corporation. Its success as a money-making machine is underlined by what Hemingway points out in the second verse: in a Polish church everything is expensive, from the robes the priests wear to the stone and ore the church is built from.

The bridge, 'Nie ma lekko, nie ma lekko, wiem na pewno, tracę tętno, Zaraz łeb mi zetną, żaden ze mnie bad boy, Tylko zły chłopiec, na którego czeka piekło' (It's not easy, it's not easy, I know for sure, I'm losing my pulse, They'll soon cut off my head, I'm no bad boy, Just a naughty boy waiting for hell), uses hyperbole to convey a sense of impending doom and personal failure. The repeated phrase 'nie ma lekko' (it's not easy) underscores the protagonist's despair and sense of inevitable punishment, reflecting the burdensome expectations placed upon him by religious teachings. In turn, Hemingway's use of direct speech and rhetorical questions further engages the listener and drives home his critiques: 'Ciekawe, że chciwość to jest jeden z grzechów głównych, co?, Gdzie miłosierdzie, kiedy tu do mnie krzyczą: "stul pysk", co?' (Interesting that greed is one of the cardinal sins, right?, Where is the mercy when they yell at me: 'shut up', right?).

Throughout the song, Hemingway employs a conversational tone and narrative style that invites the listener into his personal reflections and critiques. The cumulative effect is a condemnation of the church's abuse of power during the transition. It insinuates that the church used its considerable resources of influence to push their own agenda on Poles, who, much like the young Hemingway at the time of transition, were in a vulnerable and impressionable state. Perhaps, too, the presentation of an unequal power dynamic between a priest and a boy is a nod to the pervasive paedophilia within the Polish Catholic Church that has been exposed in recent years.

'1990s Utopia'

This topic of disillusionment with Poland's transition is continued on the track '1990s Utopia', a duet with the singer-songwriter Katarzyna Kowalczyk from the folk/electronic duo Coals, where over a spacious, almost dreamlike beat by Pejzaż and dreampop guitar, Hemingway employs similar poetic devices to previous songs, but perhaps does so more effectively.

The song opens with a series of questions that evoke memories and imagery associated with specific colours and places. However, lines like 'Pamiętasz kolor morza na Lazurowym Wybrzeżu?' (Do you remember the colour of the sea on the French Riviera?) likely come from a 1990s commercial – effectively setting the stage for the themes to come.

Thereafter, metaphors and symbols play a crucial role in highlighting the superficial nature of societal standards in capitalist Poland. For instance, the line 'Będę miał płaski brzuch, będę miał dziarski chód' (I will have a flat stomach, I will have an energetic walk) symbolizes societal standards of physical attractiveness and confidence, which seems to be emphasizing that these superficial aspects overshadow deeper values. Quite what those deeper values are, Hemingway doesn't say. Similarly, 'Biała suknia, biały uśmiech, blask gładkich nóg' (White dress, white smile, the shine of smooth legs) evokes the imagery of superficial wedding ideals.

However, this imagery contrasts sharply with the underlying reality of strained relationships and unfulfilled promises, revealing the gap between expectation and reality. For example, the stark contrast between the tender act of kissing children goodnight and the subsequent act of suicide in 'Cmokam w czoło moje dzieci, wchodzę do wrzącej wanny' (I kiss my children on the forehead, step into the boiling bath) highlights the profound disconnect between outward appearances and inner turmoil. The line 'Żyletka Gillette sunie po żyle, wypływa krew ich matki' (The Gillette razor glides along the vein, their mother's blood flows) is particularly striking.

Satire is also used to critique societal norms and expectations. For example, the line 'Chciałaś mieć żywot jak w reklamie' (You wanted a life like in an ad) highlights the unattainable and deceptive nature of the ideal life depicted in advertisements. In turn, political promises are mocked in 'Kandydat twierdzi, że znów będzie tu normalnie' (The candidate claims it will be normal here again), questioning the true meaning of 'normal' and who benefits from it.

Repetition serves to reinforce key themes and ideas. For example, the phrase 'Będę miał' (I will have) emphasizes the relentless pursuit of material and physical perfection. Similarly, 'Chciałaś mieć żywot jak w reklamie' (You wanted a life like in an ad) is repeated to underscore the pervasive influence of idealized media portrayals on individual desires and expectations.

Criticism of capitalism can also be inferred by the nods to American writer Bret Easton Ellis' novel *American Psycho*; both the '1990s Utopia' protagonist and *American Psycho*'s Patrick Bateman express a desire for a premium business card with a beautiful font. Both also have a propensity for violence. While Bateman is a serial killer who predominantly preys on women, the husband in '1990s Utopia' hits his wife. Both men have a knack for hiding their crimes; while Bateman keeps a victim's head in the freezer, the husband in '1990s Utopia' avoids his wife's face when hitting her, in this way ensuring her bruises aren't visible. And, like *American Psycho* where violence ends in killing, in '1990s Utopia' the tale also concludes in a dramatic death, though here it is the wife, rather than the husband, who causes the woman's death as she commits suicide by slitting her wrists in the bath.

That capitalism is ultimately to blame is symbolized by the mentioning of the brand of the razor she uses, Gillette, another coveted American item in capitalist Poland. It's also communicated by the fact that it is not physically the husband who kills the wife and that it is she who regales this ending, which symbolically removes some of his responsibility. Hemingway's delivery throughout is also a contrast to the violence in the song. Heavily Auto-Tuned, the husband's lines have little emotion in them. As a result, it's difficult to imagine the protagonist committing the acts described, which signals that it was his circumstances, that is, capitalism that forced him into these acts, rather than his own flawed character.

'Nie Mam Czasu' (I Don't Have Time), 'Influenza', 'Szczękościsk' (Lockjaw), 'W.N.P' (Pornography Raised Us)

On other songs on the album, Hemingway brings his criticism of capitalism up to the present moment, with songs such as the jumpy beat-accompanied 'Nie Mam Czasu' (I Don't Have Time) and the tension-building 'Influenza'. While the former references Poles' slavish devotion to consumer goods such as supplements, which promise to cure all manner of problems from weight gain to joint pain, the latter is a criticism of money-hungry celebrities who increasingly talk about topics that they don't have any knowledge about to grow their audiences and profits. While it's not the first time Hemingway has been critical of the consumerism of Poles and particularly his generation, on *Jarmark* (*Fair*) he particularly shows them as the losers of post-transition, in depicting how the supposed opportunities of market democracy haven't yielded the results that were promised.

On 'Szczękościsk' (Lockjaw), he describes how millennials are living beyond their means to show off with lines about their penchant for coffee and tapenade delivered in an accusatory tone. A vignette about a brunch meeting between friends where, despite the high bill, the diners leave a measly tip is especially effective. He also describes how education no longer delivers on the promise of a good job, as in the case of the recipient of the tip, who is stuck working as a waiter, repeatedly having to ask customers to 'enter their pin and press the green button'. The fact that the album is filled with spontaneous acts of anger is another sign that Poland is full of people who have been betrayed by market democracy.

Hemingway also uses the characters of the song to demonstrate that market democracy has resulted in class differences between Poles, as some have seemingly gotten rich, while others have remained poor, and the disdain that each group now feels for the other. This is presented through the internal thoughts of the customer in the narrative of 'Szczękościsk' (Lockjaw). He spitefully ponders on the life of the waiter serving him, wondering how the waiter spends his measly earnings and how he can afford nights out taking drugs. As these internal thoughts of the main character of the narrative suggest, and indeed the title of the song does too, 'Szczękościsk' (Lockjaw) is also a song more generally about recreational drugs. It's another element of Western-influenced consumerism that Hemingway criticises on *Jarmark* (*Fair*), describing how Poles' penchant for amphetamines is an attempt to find meaning in an increasingly vapid world where aspirational consumer goods like avocado toast hold more value than human relations.

In turn, 'W.N.P.', which stands for 'Wychowała Nas Pornografia', that is, 'Pornography Raised Us', seems to be a criticism of the influx of pornography into Poland post-transition and also a criticism of Law and Justice's stance on sex education in schools, seemingly counseling that lack of discourse on sexuality leads to citizens whose only source of sexual education is porn. This, in turn, leads to unrealistic expectations of romantic relationships and especially of women. Hemingway points out that a sex education through pornography leads men to want their partners to be both a Madonna and a whore, as illustrated by such lines as 'Chcą mieć w łożu Marię Magdalenę, co jest jednocześnie zakonnicą' (They want a Mary Magdalene in bed, who is also a nun). He suggests this creates an unrealistic fantasy world, where women are sexually insatiable while men don't need to fear any repercussions for forcing sex, and where real-life situations like a woman needing the morning-after pill and finding sex too painful never feature.

Cumulative effect of *Jarmark* (*Fair*)'s songs

One of the central themes that pervades all the songs on *Jarmark* (*Fair*) is a sense of disillusionment and discontent. This is depicted through vivid imagery of societal changes, consumerism and the characters' struggles. Another recurring theme is the exploration of identity and belonging in a rapidly changing society. The lyrics reflect on what it means to be Polish, grappling with questions of national identity and cultural heritage. The songs also offer trenchant sociopolitical commentary on contemporary Poland, addressing issues such as corruption, inequality and cultural homogenization. A key image that emerges is the cyclical nature of oppression and disillusionment. For example, in the 'Łańcuch' (Chain) trilogy, the metaphor of a chain symbolizes the interconnectedness of societal problems and the perpetuation of oppressive systems. The repetition of refrains underscores the sense of resignation and inevitability, suggesting that change is elusive and systemic problems persist.

Overall, the cumulative effect of these themes and images is a poignant portrayal of Poland, where societal changes, disillusionment and the search for meaning intersect in complex ways. The poetic devices enhance the emotional resonance of the lyrics, inviting listeners to reflect on the human experience amidst societal upheaval. However, Hemingway's use of poetic devices is often quite simple. This straightforwardness can be a double-edged sword; while it ensures clarity and accessibility, it also means that the lyrics sometimes lack the intricate wordplay and metaphorical richness that characterize more sophisticated poetry within rap. The repetition of certain phrases and motifs, while reinforcing key themes and perhaps underscoring the repetitive nature of a capitalist society, sometimes feels redundant.

Another limitation is the scarcity of personal anecdotes or more intimate storytelling, which are hallmarks of impactful hip hop and, indeed, Hemingway's previous work. On *Jarmark* (*Fair*), lyrics often remain at a more abstract level. For example, 'Polskie Tango' (Polish Tango) is a potent critique but lacks the personal touch that could make it more relatable and poignant. However, when he does refer to his own engagement with Polish society, it can feel disingenuous by virtue of him not actually living in Poland at the time of writing the album (as discussed further in Chapter 3).

The portrayal of characters and their development within the tracks is another notable issue. For example, in the 'Łańcuch' (Chain) trilogy, the characters appear more as archetypes or stereotypes rather than fully fleshed-out individuals. Moreover,

Hemingway's handling of social issues such as xenophobia and generational conflict sometimes comes across as heavy-handed. As such, some of the songs risk alienating listeners who might perceive them as overly didactic rather than thought-provoking. Additionally, the songs' rapid transitions between scenes and characters, while dynamic, sometimes result in a fragmented narrative. Indeed, there is insufficient time to fully absorb and reflect on each scenario before Hemingway moves on to the next, which is exacerbated by the fact that the 'Łańcuch' (Chain) songs are scattered throughout the album.

Finally, the fact that Hemingway offers little in terms of nuanced solutions or hope for change on any of the songs on the album can also be viewed as problematic. The album makes one wonder what, if anything, Hemingway believes in. On *Jarmark* (*Fair*) he's anti-Catholic, anti-capitalist, frustrated and fatalistic. Moreover, by boiling issues down to binaries, Hemingway fails to communicate that Polish history is often self-contradictory, with its embrace of both capitalism and traditional values. It leaves the listener wondering whether this simplification is the culmination of his position as an outsider who emigrated and thus seemingly lost his grip on the nuances of his country.

Colonizer or colonized? *Jarmark* (*Fair*)'s western musical influences

The term 'colonialism' refers to a specific form of domination and exploitation with political, economic and cultural dimensions. Some commentators emphasize its cultural aspects, while others stress economic and/or political characteristics (Mazierska et al. 2014: 3). Art historian Jaak Kangilaski highlights that the most important characteristic of colonialism is the cultural and ethnic difference between the colonizer and the colonized, as well as the perception of the colonizer's language and culture as superior (Mazierska et al. 2014: 3). As such, what defines colonialism is not a set of (legal) characteristics but the economic, political, cultural and socio-psychological nature of colonialism in its entirety (Mazierska et al. 2014: 3).

Scholars also point to different types of colonialism. According to scholar Anne McClintock, there are three types: (1) colonization, which involves taking over another territory and exploiting its resources, interfering with its power structure; (2) internal colonization, which happens when a dominant part of a country treats a group or region like a foreign colony; and (3) imperial colonization, which is large-scale territorial domination of the kind that gave late Victorian Britain and Europe control over 85 per cent of the earth, and the USSR totalitarian rule over Hungary, Poland and Czechoslovakia in the twentieth century (McClintock 1992, cited by Mazierska et al. 2014: 5).

To understand Poland's relationship to colonization, we need to look at its past. Throughout the second half of the twentieth century, while economically colonized by the USSR, 'Poland enjoyed, by and large, a privileged position within the Eastern Bloc, being able to retain many of its cultural and social privileges, such as a strong Catholic Church and largely private agriculture and being rewarded rather than punished for the acts of rebellion against the political status quo' (Mazierska et al. 2014: 8). Indeed, during communism, Poland enjoyed greater freedom than other countries from the Soviet Bloc, with many Western goods such as jeans and cultural products such as books, films and music entering Poland much faster than other Soviet Bloc countries. As such, 'readers in Warsaw Pact countries with stricter censorship than Poland often first encountered many American authors in Polish translation' (Delaney and Antoszek 2017: 78). This is perhaps why following the fall of communism in 1989, Poland, through joining NATO in 1999 and the EU in 2004, quite easily shifted from its position as an Eastern European country, to one more closely aligned with the West as a member of the newly drawn Central Europe.

However, despite this integration, scholars such as József Böröcz (2009) draw on world-systems theory to argue that countries of Central-Eastern Europe, including Poland, are not equal to the Western European countries of the EU. This theory, developed by sociologist Immanuel Wallerstein, divides the world into core, semi-periphery and periphery nations. Core countries are dominant, economically diversified and technologically advanced. They exploit periphery countries, which are less developed and provide raw materials and labour. Semi-periphery countries fall in between, having characteristics of both core and periphery. Poland, as a semi-periphery, Böröcz argues, still faces economic dependencies and political pressures from core nations in Western Europe. In turn, in *Border as Method*, political scientists Sandro Mezzadra and Brett Neilson (2013) show that, despite borders ostensibly being more malleable and freedom of movement made easier in places like the EU, borders and new exploitative subjectivities are on the rise, being created and maintained via the legal system and restricted access to labour markets.

Another viewpoint is that a certain 'self-colonization' followed Poland's transition from socialism to market democracy. This is sometimes described as individuals 'traumatizing' themselves in relation to the West by willingly adopting its values (Samaluk 2016: 100). When it comes to popular music, scholars often say Eastern Europe was culturally dominated by Western, mainly Anglo-American, music even before communism fell (Mazierska 2023: 309). Historian Timothy Ryback points out Beatlemania in Poland, East Germany and the Czech Republic as an example, arguing that Western rock culture debunked Marxist-Leninist assumptions about the state's ability to control its citizens as young socialists who should have been bonded by the liturgy of Marx and Lenin instead found common ground in the music of the Rolling Stones and The Beatles (Ryback cited in Mazierska 2023a: 309).

Poland's embracing of hip hop, if not self-colonization, can also be characterized as an adoption of Western culture and values, not least because Poland's early hip hop had much in common with its American antecedent. For example, Polish rap pioneer Liroy sampled A Tribe Called Quest, Cypress Hill and Public Enemy on his first album *Alboom* (*Album*) and peppered his raps with English words and phrases such as 'fucking' (Lech 2023) while other American hip hop slang words such as 'the yard', 'homies', 'yo' and 'bitches' were translated into Polish, 'creating some rather comic borrowings: *podwórko*, *kolesie*, *trzym się*, and *foki*' (Delaney and Antoszek 2017: 84).

When it comes to Taco Hemingway's *Jarmark* (*Fair*), alignment with western music is chiefly expressed through the album's sound. The songs, although all original compositions, sound familiar. Their song structures are reminiscent of contemporary hip hop, R&B, pop and even metal music, with the beats sounding like they could have been made for artists like pop star Dua Lipa or R&B icon Rihanna. Such a reading aligns with what Hemingway's producers have said. One of Hemingway's chief beatmakers, Borucci, admits in an October 2020 interview that he watches what western artists do, and copies it. He gives the example of Drake's 'Control', which he said he was inspired by for Hemingway's track 'Wiatr' (Wind) on the EP *Wosk* (*Wax*), saying, 'They were the same chords – I just changed the order' (Szufladowicz 2020). Hemingway's '6 zer' (6 zeros) has also been criticized for sounding too much like Drake. Reviewing *Jarmark* (*Fair*), critics too pointed to the album's lack of distinctiveness, praising the producers for their technical ability but also pointing out that they failed to create a uniquely Polish sound.

With all songs in minor keys, the album's melancholy is reminiscent of American rapper Kanye West's 2008 album *808s & Heartbreak*, also by virtue of its frequent use of Auto-Tune, which was first popularized by West and other American rappers like T-Pain, and later extensively used by American rappers Travis Scott and Future. Much like in his previous work, Hemingway continues to reference the American hip hop subgenres of trap and drill. He also explicitly pays homage to American hip hop artists, as in the nod to Brooklyn drill artist Pop Smoke. Hemingway's 'POL Smoke' bears similarity to Pop Smoke's track 'Dior' due to its very similar melody line. It also pays homage via the song's title, which can be read as Hemingway describing himself as the Polish Pop Smoke, given that the letters 'POL' in the title can be read as an abbreviation of 'Polish'.

The production on *Jarmark* (*Fair*) also follows the shift in western hip hop towards increasingly lower frequencies. Since its inception, the frequency range of hip hop has shifted lower and lower, to the point where you would need high-end equipment to hear the low end on many productions today. Released in 1991, A Tribe Called Quest's album *The Low End Theory* was a statement on the role of bass frequencies in music, especially hip hop, and how bass can act as the foundation of the beat. It still sounds good through the speakers of an iPhone. But fast forward thirty years, and synthetic bass sounds processed with digital EQ and high compression have enabled a kind of low-frequency race to the bottom. Bass can be lower and can be pushed a lot higher in the mix. Still, most fans won't have the speakers needed to hear it, and as such, Hemingway's decision to follow this route can be read as a purely artistic choice to demonstrate, not least to himself, that he is on equal footing with his western counterparts.

Such a reading is strengthened by the fact that the Stadion Dziesięciolecia (10th-Anniversary Stadium) *Jarmark* (*Fair*)'s title also alludes to, and the very concept of 'a fair', is a place where fare from different countries is displayed side by side, on an even footing, each fighting for the attention and appreciation of potential customers. It brings to mind the concept of aesthetic cosmopolitanism, as developed by sociologist Motti Regev. Regev sees pop-rock (an umbrella term encompassing pop, rock, electronic music and hip hop, among other styles) as expressing the cultural logic of late modernity and consisting of intensified aesthetic proximity, overlap and connectivity between nations and ethnicities. It is a process in which the expressive forms of cultural practices used by nations at large (and by groupings within them), to signify and perform their sense of uniqueness, come to share large proportions of aesthetic common ground, to a point where the cultural uniqueness of each nation or ethnicity cannot but be understood as a unit within one complex entity, one variant in a set of quite similar (although never identical) cases (Regev 2013: 3).

As popular music scholar Ewa Mazierska notes, when applying the concept of aesthetic cosmopolitanism to Eastern European popular music of the state socialist period, there are distinct advantages of using this concept in such a context. The main one consists of seeing Eastern European popular music as a form of global pop-rock, rather than an imitation (Mazierska 2016: 5). Of course, if we apply the concept of aesthetic cosmopolitanism to Eastern European pop-rock from the state socialist period, there is even more reason to use this term to examine Polish popular music after 1989. No doubt, by naming his record *Jarmark* (*Fair*), Hemingway encourages us to read his work as participating in global cultural trends. However, perhaps he's also simultaneously mocking Poles' (and, possibly, his own) ambition to overcome their provinciality. This is because Stadion Dziesięciolecia (10th-Anniversary Stadium) was also a byword for kitsch, resulting from the fact that a large proportion of fare displayed there consisted of pirated and low-quality products, including cassettes with disco polo music.

Arguably not intentionally, the album's rollout gives credence to reading *Jarmark* (*Fair*) as a cheap imitation of western music because the album's cover was accused of plagiarizing the work of American photographer Alex Prager. In response, the creators of the *Jarmark* (*Fair*) artwork issued a statement that they consciously drew inspiration from the work of various photographers, including Prager, with the aim being to translate the style of America of the 1960s into the Polish realities of the 1990s. They said they regretted not making this explicit when the *Jarmark* (*Fair*) cover was revealed, noting the inspiration would be highlighted in the album's physical version (Oleksiak 2020). Eventually, the artwork, which depicted a 24-hour store shop front, with various representatives of Polish society – from small traders to a nun, a binman and a policeman – depicted as going about their daily lives with Hemingway in the centre, was changed to a side profile shot of Hemingway with an image of tropical fruits as the backdrop.

There is also another interpretation to consider. As pointed out by academics Kate Delaney and Andrzej Antoszek, enthusiasm for American cultural products pre-1989 and after the fall of communism waned with Poland's populist turn. They point to the popularity of nationalist parties like the League of Polish Families (Liga Polskich Rodzin) and Self Defence (Samoobrona), which reject America as a symbol of globalization and modernization, viewing it as a threat to Polish culture (Delaney and Antoszek 2017: 87). As such, *Jarmark* (*Fair*)'s adoption of western hip hop elements can be read as a protest against Poland's populism and nationalism.

Most likely, Hemingway's biggest desire was for *Jarmark* (*Fair*) to be seen as evidence of him being a serious international musician fully participating in global music trends. Such a reading is strengthened by the fact that by the end of *Jarmark* (*Fair*) Hemingway has 'checked out' of Poland, signaled by the album ending with a verse from Artur Rojek, not Hemingway himself. It's also demonstrated by the fact that Hemingway seems to be looking westwards on *Jarmark* (*Fair*)'s sister record *Europa* (*Europe*) where he more or less leaves the topic of Poland, focusing on himself and his problems, and fills the tracks with references to Europe.

3 Social remittances, the reception of the album and the failure of the 'Grand Narrative' of Polish migration

In this chapter, I will reflect on *Jarmark* (*Fair*)'s impact and reception. I'll discuss it as a document that critiques the 'Grand Narrative of Polish migration', while also highlighting the influence migrants can have, known as social remittances. I will particularly focus on the timing of the album's release during a critical point of potential change in Polish politics. I will examine its critical, media and commercial reception, as well as the album's accolades, such as Fryderyk awards. Additionally, I'll analyse the album's afterlife by examining how it has influenced Polish music and society since its release.

Social remittances – criticism of Poland in Hemingway's work through the lens of migration

Hemingway's work can be understood in terms of how migration affects countries of origin, including economically, socially and culturally. Sociologist Peggy Levitt coined the term 'social remittances' to describe the norms, practices, identities and social capital flowing from migrants back to their home countries (Levitt 1998: 927; Levitt and Lamba-Nieves 2011: 3). She argues that they're an important aspect of migration to study because they 'travel through identifiable pathways to specific audiences, policymakers and planners [which] can channel certain kinds of information to particular groups with positive results' (Levitt 1998: 927).

Social remittances occur when migrants return home or when stayers visit their migrant friends and family members, as well as through other means of communication, such as through letters and telephone calls (Levitt 1998: 936). They can be transmitted by individuals, organizations or informal networks (Levitt 1998: 936; Levitt and Lamba-Nieves 2011: 2). Circulating between migrants and non-migrants, social remittances can influence each group's experiences and behaviours (Levitt and Lamba-Nieves 2011: 3). Levitt also writes that social remittance transmission differs from other types of global culture dissemination, in that it is identifiable, while it's more difficult to track how global cultures emerge and diffuse (Levitt 1998: 937).

Social remittances affect family life, work and politics (Jarvinen-Alenius et al., quoted in Krzyżowski 2016: 74) though various factors influence the transmission of social remittances, including ease of travel and communication, migrants' economic roles and their social and political standing in their new countries (Levitt 1998: 928). Research also shows that the level of transmission depends on migrants' networks and the diversity of those networks (Krzyżowski 2016: 82). Crucially, they can lead to regional and national changes (Levitt and Deepak Lamba-Nieve 2011: 1) and contribute to social change and consolidation, especially when transmitted through diverse networks (Grabowska 2018: 69).

While for most of his career Hemingway has ignored calls for him to make music that engages with Polish politics, rapping on 'Wosk' (Wax) that he is 'the voice of a generation who has nothing to say' ('Jestem głosem pokolenia, które nie ma nic do powiedzenia') and that while he hears calls for him to be more political, he would rather rap about himself: 'Ktoś wywołał mnie, bym pisał teksty polityczne, Nie, dziękuję, Wolę pisać o sobie' (Someone called on me to write political texts, No, thank you, I prefer to write about myself) on *Jarmark* (*Fair*) he changed tack. This is likely because of Law and Justice. In the lead up to the 2020 presidential election – which they presented as a battle to save the Polish 'traditional' family against the onslaught of modernity – they doubled-down on their populist rightwing ideologies of traditionalism, religiosity and nativism (Zbytniewska 2022).

Hemingway's approach on this record can be conceptualized as social remittances as described by scholar Devesh Kapur (2008) whose research examines local-global linkages in political and economic change. According to him, 'migrants reshape politics through three channels of departure, return and involvement from afar changing the balance of power among different social groups, championing or thwarting policy initiatives, and weakening or strengthening political institutions' (Kapur, quoted in Levitt and Lamba-Nieves 2011: 6).

Attempting to change the power structure among social groups can be described as the mission of tracks such as

'Łańcuch I: Kiosk' (Chain 1: Kiosk), where, as discussed in Chapter 2, Hemingway describes xenophobia towards immigrants, especially those from Ukraine. He does this via the aforementioned vignette about an Uber passenger who Hemingway reveals doesn't trust drivers with names such as Sasha and Dimitri, in this way forcing Poles to face their own prejudices. His portrayal of an unhappy marriage on '1990s Utopia' is an even bolder attempt. It can be read as a criticism of the powerful Catholic Church in Poland, and the resulting social stigma of divorce.

Thwarting policy initiatives can be said to be the aim of 'Polskie Tango' (Polish Tango) because here Hemingway describes Poland as a country ruled by a propaganda of fear and one where Law and Justice has bribed its citizens via handouts. This can be inferred from the comparison of Poland to Santa Claus, bringing to the listener's attention the fact that Poland's flag has the same colours as depictions of the fictional Christmas character. It seems that Hemingway is likening the Law and Justice PLN 500 child benefit to that of Santa Claus giving out gifts, suggesting that Poles are like children, that is, people who can be easily bribed. He continues this characterization with the line 'Główną misją dla nich mówić ci, że żyjesz świetnie' (Their main mission is to tell you that you are living great), underlining that Law and Justice are winning over voters through propaganda. Another line that makes this point is 'Tylko ty masz rację – reszta świata żyje w błędzie' (Only you are right – the rest of the world is wrong), which again likens Law and Justice voters to children by suggesting they're not only bribed by handouts but also seemingly won over by shallow praise. Law and Justice's supposed strategy of dumbing down their electorate is also called out by the line 'Patrz trochę węziej, patrz trochę węziej' (Look a little narrower, look a little narrower), a subversion of a song by the rapper Łona. However, perhaps the strongest indication that 'Polskie Tango' (Polish Tango) was a direct attack on Law and Justice was the inclusion of the eight-star symbol of the Ruch Ośmiu Gwiazd, an anti-Law and Justice campaign in the track's video. Its name, 'Jebać PiS', which translates as 'Fuck Law and Justice', became a widely used meme during the presidential campaign.

In turn, Hemingway's criticism of the Law and Justice position on gender can be inferred from the traditional gender roles of the protagonists of '1990s Utopia'; while the man goes out to work, the woman stays home and looks after the children and the house. Given that that their unhappy union ends in the woman's suicide, one can infer that Hemingway is criticizing a political regime where a marriage between a man and a woman and the nuclear family is the idealized norm. The last two lines of the song are also telling: 'The candidate says it's going to be normal here again, But what will this normal be like? And who will it be for?' (Kandydat twierdzi, że znów będzie tu normalnie, Lecz jaka ta normalność ma być? Dla kogo być?) he sings, referencing the Law and Justice campaign ahead of the 2020 presidential election, where the party's message was that Poland needed to be rescued from the dangers of the Western norms of the European Union, to return it to the 'normalcy' of traditional family values. Finally, criticism of the Law and Justice stance on traditional gender roles can also be deduced from 'W.N.P', that is, 'Wychowała Nas Pornografia' (Pornography Raised Us), whose message, as described in

Chapter 2, is that lack of discourse on sexuality leads to citizens whose only source of sexual education is porn, which in turn leads to unrealistic expectations of romantic relationships, especially of women. Meanwhile, on 'Panie, to Wyście!' (Sir, it's You!) Hemingway brings to attention the perceived social divide in Poland, which is often cited as the reason for the success of Law and Justice, who have introduced policies favourable to those living in rural areas. His lyrics imply that the divide is a false narrative, peddled to serve those in power.

Hemingway also points to the difficulties Law and Justice's policies have created for those who are different in Poland, not least for Hemenway himself, as he points to the anger his opinions give rise to on 'Panie, to Wyście!' (Sir, it's You!). It's a trope he continues on *Jarmark* (*Fair*)'s sister record *Europa* (*Europe*) where on 'WWA Nie Berlin' (WWA Not Berlin) he tells his listeners: 'Chcesz być inny, to pocierpisz, Będzie wpierdol, bo Warszawa to nie Berlin' (If you wanna be different, you'll suffer, They'll beat you up, because Warsaw isn't Berlin). That Hemingway is trying to foster greater tolerance towards the LGBT community with this track makes sense, given that this is one social remittance that is quite common among return migrants in Poland. 'Demonstrations in support of refugee or LGBT rights in Poland regularly involve Polish return migrants alongside stayers', write White et al. (2018: 27), while adding that 'Polish LGBT activists such as Robert Biedroń, Poland's first gay mayor, gained inspiration from periods of living and working in other EU countries' (2018: 27).

A more cosmopolitan outlook, or a certain 'wokeness' and a desire to educate Poles on its virtues, is evident throughout the 'lessons' of *Jarmark* (*Fair*) and is also evident on several tracks on *Europa* (*Europe*), such as 'Toskania Outro' (Tuscany Outro). First, the track's title refers to the Italian region of Tuscany, home to some of the world's most recognizable Renaissance art and architecture, in this way suggesting that Hemingway is himself also an intellectual and modernizer. Second, he makes it clear that he's attempting to change Poles' outlook on issues such as toxic masculinity by rapping: 'Staram się redefiniować męskość, Chcę nauczyć typów, że to super kiedy tęsknią, Że nie muszą dusić kiedy uprawiają seks z nią, Że gdy na agresję odpowiada się agresją' (I'm trying to redefine masculinity, I want to teach guys that it's cool to miss someone, that it's not necessary to choke a woman when they're having sex with her, that you don't meet aggression with aggression). The pitfalls of toxic masculinity is also the topic of the 2018 Bedoes and Kubi Producent track on which he features, 'Chłopaki nie płaczą' (Boys don't cry), which counsels especially against macho violence. Meanwhile, there is also a more subtle attempt of conveying cosmopolitanism via brands mentioned. According to Miszczynski and Tomaszewski (2017: 146), Polish rap has traditionally fostered classlessness and collective solidarity through its use of brands. It also shaped a new self-perception within the context of Polish neoliberal reality by avoiding ostentatious consumption and emphasizing the equality between rappers and their audience (2017: 152). However, Hemingway's trajectory appears to differ as his career progresses. He increasingly incorporates foreign brands into his work, possibly signalling a growing gap between him and his Polish audience, or aiming to introduce them to a wider array of products and fashion styles. For example, on

Europa (*Europe*)'s 'Big Pharma' he namechecks brands such as the French skincare line Bioderma, the French leather luxury brand Celine and the celebrity favourite Fiji Water, which was founded by a Canadian businessman.

Hemingway is also critical of Poles more directly, and particularly his fans, in tracks such as '8 kobiet' (8 women) from his 2018 album *Soma 0,5 mg* with Quebonafide. Conveying his supposed cosmopolitanism and his fans' lack thereof by pointing out a fan's mispronunciation of the Canadian rapper Tory Lanez's name, the track's title also seemingly speaks to Hemingway's worldliness, being a nod to the dark comedy *8 women*, by French film director François Ozon. Hemingway also describes his fans as wolves elsewhere on the track, recounting how they relentlessly ask him to autograph their phone cases and for photos.

Hemingway's low opinion of Polish institutions can also be gleaned from his approach to the media and his disregard for Polish accolades. He famously doesn't give interviews to journalists, nor has he personally accepted any of the Fryderyk music awards he's received. On '100 km/h' from *Umowa o dzieło* (*Contract work*), he even explicitly says that he would rather receive a Nobel Prize than a Fryderyk, a subject he returns to on *Marmur* (*Marble*)'s 'Ślepe sumy' (Blind sums). Here, he mentions coveting a Nobel Prize once more, as well as the American Grammy. That this standpoint is a disregard for Polish institutions is underlined by the fact that following *Jarmark* (*Fair*)'s release Hemingway gave an interview to the American newspaper the *New York Times*, telling the interviewer that his parents 'wouldn't forgive me if I said no' (Marshall 2020). Within this context, it's also important to mention that earlier in his career, Hemingway was active on the website Genius, a 2009 founded site which allows users to provide annotations and interpretation to song lyrics. He would either co-sign interpretations he agreed with, or provide clarifications, should some explanations be incorrect. Such a micromanaging approach pertaining to his message, while avoiding the media, can be understood as a clear attempt to influence social groups from afar.

A more critical view is to see Hemingway's criticism of Poles and Poland throughout his work but particularly on *Jarmark* (*Fair*) as an attempt to 'colonize' Poles with Western millennial values, particularly the rejection of capitalism. That a rejection of capitalism is a growing trend is illustrated by recent reports which have found that millennials in the United Kingdom are a hyper-politicized generation, which embraces 'woke', progressive and anti-capitalist ideas (Niemietz 2021: 6), with similar findings about Gen Z. A similar picture emerges from the United States: according to the American think tank Pew Research Centre, just 40 per cent of those aged eighteen to twenty-nine view capitalism positively – the lowest share in any age group and 33 percentage points lower than the share of those sixty-five and older (Pew Research Centre 2022: 7). Given his position as a resident of the United Kingdom, which he seemed to have been prior and after writing *Jarmark* (*Fair*) (Marshall 2020) and the overwhelmingly didactic quality of its lyrics on the album, it's arguably fair to say Hemingway was indeed imposing his UK-honed views on the supposedly capitalism-loving Poland.

The measure of social remittances – critical reception, commercial success and the 'Grand Narrative' of Polish migration

In a 2015 *Vice* article that asked fans what they like about Hemingway's music, responses leaned towards the idea that Hemingway symbolized a fresh perspective in Polish music and that his songs resonated with people who weren't typically rap fans (Wolniaczyk and Piasecki 2015). His lyrics were singled out as speaking to and for a new generation of Poles. It's a surmation that's continued to typify reception to his music throughout Hemingway's career. One YouTube fan, writing about his feature on fellow Polish rapper Schafter's 2019 track 'Bigos' (Hunter's stew), made the comment that while someone like Polish rapper Bedoes might be featured in a video drinking on a park bench, Hemingway is shown cutting up an avocado, which aligns him with the lifestyles of millennials and Gen Z (Wernio 2017). However, with each new release after his Polish debut *Trójkąt warszawski* (*Warsaw triangle*), Hemingway was less favourably viewed. While albums such as *Umowa o dzieło* (*Contract work*) and *Marmur* (*Marble*) were still praised and Hemingway's technical ability was deemed to have improved, he was accused of less intelligent rhymes, and a lack of original material (Flint 2016; Kmiecik 2016; Samborski 2019). Hemingway was also criticized for being increasingly self-obsessed; too many of his tracks were focused on his dissatisfaction with his life as an ever more famous rapper and not enough space was given to sociological observations.

When Hemingway released 'Polskie Tango' (Polish Tango) critics pointed to the fact that the political nature of the song, which they identified as a criticism of Poland and Law and Justice, was an about turn for Hemingway, who previously refused to write politically charged songs. It was no coincidence, they surmised, that the song dropped two days before the presidential election. That this was an effective tactic was underlined by pointing out that the song quickly broke Hemingway's previous record for streams achieved in the space of twenty-four hours (Muzyk 2020). Given how different it was to his previous material, 'Polskie Tango' (Polish Tango) was understood as a taste of more of the same on the forthcoming *Jarmark* (*Fair*) album, and it was eagerly awaited by critics and fans alike.

Hemingway released *Jarmark (Fair)* on 28 August 2020 by which point Andrzej Duda had won the presidential election. Reviews of the album were mixed. Critics predominantly praised a handful of songs at the beginning of the album – especially strong was the 'Łańcuch' (Chain) trilogy, most argued, and the album's other songs featuring other artists, like '1990s Utopia' with vocals from Coals' Katarzyna Kowalczyk. Praised too were the album's producers. But most critics found more to criticize than commend the album for, noting their expectation for politicized lyrics following 'Polskie Tango' (Polish Tango), which failed to materialize. It was also noted that Hemingway seemed to be focusing on social commentary rather than offering further criticism of Law and Justice, or indeed any answers to the country's problems. Hemingway was also accused of a broad strokes approach to this line of attack. For example, writing in the music and culture publication Noizz, music critic

Jan Tracz accused Hemingway of not making the effort to look beyond his own narrow worldview, nor to encourage his listeners, characterized usually as mostly young city-dwelling professionals working in corporations, to do the same (Tracz 2020). *Jarmark* (*Fair*), Tracz concluded, was a Hemingway album that would go down in history as 'just another Taco Hemingway album', to be relegated to his least noteworthy work, much like the equally forgettable *Café Belga*. Much better, according to Tracz, was Hemingway's *POCZTÓWKA Z WWA, LATO '19 (POSTCARD FROM WWA*, (SUMMER'19) LP where Hemingway's focus is his hometown of Warsaw and his own interiority. It was a point echoed by Noizz's then-editor Oliwia Botomswe, who also argued that Hemingway was much more effective when writing about the lives of young Varsovians, than trying to comment on the state of the nation (Botomswe 2020), which she described as tabloid-style commentary that landed particularly badly owing to the pop-leaning music of the album. A similar conclusion came from Rafał Samborski writing on prominent news portal Interia, who described the album as one for listeners under eighteen years of age – anyone else, he believed, wouldn't find anything revelatory in Hemingway's lyrics (Samborski 2020). Hip hop critic Miłosz Beśka (2020) also accused Hemingway of pointing out the obvious about Polish society, writing that the album's themes could be summarised as criticism of the church for being money grabbing and its protection of paedophiles, criticism of politicians for their lies, criticism of the state for stealing from citizens and criticism of citizens for their complaining nature. *Jarmark* (*Fair*), Beśka argued, would have been a far more interesting album had it focused on issues like the climate crisis, the mass immigration of young people from Poland and Poland's reliance on other countries. In focusing on those more obvious subjects, Hemingway was taking a shortcut. This was also the overall conclusion of hip hop critic Bartłomiej Ciepłota (2020) writing in popular rap publication Glamrap, who summarized *Jarmark* (*Fair*) as an album that was rushed, and as such, one characterized by generalizations and lyrical fillers, which he described as a disappointing, boring listen.

Commentators on YouTube also found issue with *Jarmark* (*Fair*), with the popular music focused channel kultura niska describing the album as one that tried to cover too many topics, which resulted in none being discussed with any depth. According to the YouTuber, the album lacked a certain lightness, taking itself too seriously, while the music itself lacked coherence (kultura niska 2020). Popular culture YouTubers Włodek Markowicz and Karol Paciorek, who present under the moniker Lekko Stronniczy, made the same assessment as music critics in describing the album as one made up of subject matter gleaned from headlines. The result, they said, was that Hemingway raps about things that don't impact him personally, which feels inauthentic and lacks impact. Lekko Stronniczy also accused Hemingway of too much moralizing without enough storytelling to back it up – citing the drug-focused song 'POL Smoke' as an example (Lekko Stronniczy 2020).

Some non-Polish-speaking YouTubers also reviewed songs from *Jarmark* (*Fair*), particularly 'Polskie Tango' (Polish Tango) which they noted had high viewing figures. For example, the Indian YouTuber V-nesh (2020) and his friends who feature in the review praised Hemingway for his flow and music, saying their inability to understand Polish didn't diminish their enjoyment of the song, though they made an effort to decipher the lyrics' meaning by translating them. But some YouTubers, such as one posting under the alias Nirav Reactions, didn't understand what Hemingway was talking about, mistaking Hemingway's comments about the West as commentary on the Soviet Union (Nirav Reactions 2020). In comments, a fan wrote in response that perhaps Hemingway's subject matter was too Poland-specific.

The overall lacklustre reception was shot through by critics pointing to Hemingway writing *Jarmark* (*Fair*) while living in London, and so, seemed far removed from what was going on in Poland. Bosomtwe (2020), in particular, underlined that such a position undermined any comparison of Hemingway to Poland's great poets; the only legitimate comparison to Norwid, she argued, was that Hemingway continued to be a migrant in the physical sense. She also disparaged him as someone who'd absconded from his responsibilities as a public figure, choosing only to partake in public life via his music. As such, one can read *Jarmark* (*Fair*) as another testament of Hemingway's failure and the failure of the 'Grand Narrative' of Polish migration. Not only had he not made it in the West, but Hemingway had returned to Poland intellectually impoverished – having no grip on the nuances of what was going on in his home country.

Hemingway appeared to take note. Known for diligently releasing music every summer, after *Jarmark* (*Fair*) and *Europa* (*Europe*), Hemingway went quiet. Summers came and went, but Hemingway failed to release a new solo record. When he did re-emerge, it was as a featured artist on projects by a new generation of Polish artists, such as Mata's *Młody Matczak* (*Young Matczak*) debut album and the group 2115's *RODZINNY BIZNES* (*FAMILY BUSINESS*). It seemed as if Hemingway had taken the lacklustre reception to *Jarmark* (*Fair*) to heart and potentially he was done with music, or at least was having a break. On 2115's 'DRESSCODE' he described his domestic situation – moving into a new flat with his girlfriend, rather than making any allusions to a comeback.

In the meantime, the new generation of Gen Z rappers cited him as an inspiration. For example, the son of a well-known lawyer (Bandosz 2022: 28), Mata, said it was thanks to Hemingway that he felt that there was a place for him (as someone from a middle-class background) on the Polish hip hop scene. He also said Hemingway's storytelling technique and subject matter turned the scene upside down. Mata even gave an interview to the same *New York Times* writer, who Hemingway agreed to an interview with following the release of *Jarmark* (*Fair*), which can be read as wanting to follow in Hemingway's footsteps.

As the years rolled by, Hemingway's fans' anticipation grew. A whole movement, embodied by comments on social media and memes, focused around the wait for a new album. Eventually, in December 2022, Hemingway came back as part of a multi-generational collective of rappers who began releasing music under the moniker club2020, where Hemingway was front and centre, even appearing in the group's debut video and accompanying behind-the-scenes documentary. Listening to the collective's songs, you could immediately sense that Hemingway's passion for rap was back. Still, his verses lacked depth and the overall vibe of the project was more commercial than his other output.

On 22 September 2023, the official last day of summer, Hemingway dropped his new solo project, *1-800-Oświecenie* (*1-800-Enlightenment*), a concept album on which Hemingway plays the role of a late-night radio host. In the interludes between songs, he talks to listeners who call in and confide about their problems. Music critics interpreted the album as an attempt at therapy. The songs discuss topics such as transience, nostalgia for one's youth, disappointment with adulthood, mental health, addictions, consumerism and the need to achieve 'enlightenment'. Perhaps, the critical failure of *Jarmark* (*Fair*) had taken its toll. What was clear was that Hemingway had given up on trying to educate the nation.

Still, for all its shortcomings, as mentioned in Chapter 1, *Jarmark* (*Fair*) sold well. Hemingway deputed at number one on the OLiS (Official Sales Chart) for a fifth consecutive year with *Jarmark* (*Fair*), while *Europa* (*Europe*) came second. Together with his other albums, Hemingway had equaled Czesław Niemen's record for the number of albums in one OLiS listing. The album was certified gold on 24 September 2020. It also boasts its Fryderyk successes.

Conclusion – after *Jarmark* (*Fair*) and the album's afterlife

That Hemingway has changed Polish music is undeniable. When Spotify launched in Poland, the site's top ten artists in the country were all international acts, with international rock bands being streamed the most. In fact, there were only five Polish artists on the entire Top 100 list that year. But, as Mateusz Smółka, Spotify Music Team Lead for Eastern Europe, said in a 2023 interview, Hemingway played a leading role in changing Poles' streaming habits. 'Looking back, international artists controlled the top three spots until about 2017. But in 2018, we saw the rise of Polish artists, most notably when the Taco Hemingway and Quebonafide collaboration Taconafide, and Dawid Podsiadło took the top spots. Since then, Polish artists have been in the Top 10 each year, with 76 Polish songs making the local Top 100 in 2022' (Spotify 2023). Polish rap dominates, as demonstrated by the popularity of Spotify's local flagship hip hop playlist RAP GENERACJA (RAP GENERATION), which has been the number one playlist in Poland every year since its launch (Spotify 2023).

In 2023, the music of Polish artists witnessed an even bigger increase, going up by 18 per cent in comparison to the previous year. The top ten artists list was dominated by homegrown talent, with only one foreign artist, The Weeknd, making the cut. The list was led by Hemingway who was Spotify's most streamed artist in Poland that year. His collaborative club2020 project and his solo album *1-800-Oświecenie* (*1-800-Enlightenment*) were in the top three most listened to albums and *1-800-Oświecenie* (*1-800-Enlightenment*) broke the record for the highest number of streams on Spotify among Polish users in one day. It also debuted at the top of the OLiS physical albums and OLiS streamed albums sales charts. To date, it has been certified double platinum, selling 60,000 copies, making it one of Hemingway's best-selling records so far.

This trajectory echoes a glocalization trend seen across the European music market. The latest findings from the International Federation of the Phonographic Industry's 2023 Global Music Report note that 'there was an acceleration in the popularity of local repertoire in 2022, a trend that has become more prevalent as streaming has grown to be the largest global format by revenue' (Page and Dalla Riva 2023: 23). Across fifty-three official national single charts overseen or monitored by the IFPI, artists local to that market took the top spot in twenty-seven markets (Page and Dalla Riva 2023: 23).

With the exception of Spanish-speaking acts, this doesn't translate to local acts finding fandom outside the borders of their countries though. The same goes for Polish hip hop. While some point to Polish being phonetically inaccessible to foreigners, even compared to other Slavic languages, because Polish has a lot of so-called rustling sounds, which makes Polish sound like 'white noise from a TV or wind during a violent storm' (Kempiński 2023), the situation could likely be improved if scholars of Polish music gave more consideration to Polish hip hop. However, contemporary Polish hip hop especially is rather marginalized within the scholarship of Polish popular music, with most studies (e.g. *Made in Poland*, 2020, ed. Patryk Galuszka) focusing on historical studies at the expense of more contemporary phenomena, while privileging folk, rock and punk.

But what of *Jarmark* (*Fair*)? How big a role has this particular album played in Hemingway's endurance, still dominating the Polish music market ten years into his career? And what of its wider sociocultural impact? In answer to this question, one could turn to Poland's October 2023 elections when seats in both the lower house, the Sejm, and the Senate, were being contested. At the previous 2019 parliamentary election, Law and Justice had held onto its majority in the Sejm with the Prime Minister Mateusz Morawiecki forming a second government. In the lead up to the 2023 election, opposition leader and former prime minister Donald Tusk, led the Civic Coalition (Koalicja Obywatelska) political alliance in opposition to Law and Justice.

Opposition parties asserted that the very essence of democracy hung in the balance, framing the electoral contest as a pivotal moment. In contrast, Law and Justice characterised the election as a decisive dichotomy, portraying it as a choice between Poland succumbing to EU pressure to open its borders to undocumented migrants and embracing a pro-LGBT agenda, or embracing an autonomous government committed to securing Poland's borders and upholding Christian traditions.

YouTube comments on 'Polskie Tango' (Polish Tango) drew attention to how apt the song still was and that its message hit harder than when it was originally released. Many viewers had returned to the song to give them strength through the stress of the election, while others drew attention to the fact the video had been watched 38 million times, the exact number of Poles currently living in Poland, underlining its impact.

When votes of the election were counted, the results were at first inconclusive. While the United Right (Zjednoczona Prawica) alliance secured the most seats, it fell short of a Sejm majority. The opposition, represented by the Civic Coalition, Third Way (Trzecia Droga) and The Left (Lewica), amassed a combined vote share of 54 per cent, which almost a month later culminated in the formation of a majority coalition government. In the Senate, the opposition electoral alliance Senate Pact 2023 (Pakt Senacki 2023) clinched both a plurality of the vote and a majority of seats. As such, one can deduce that although ultimately Law and Justice lost their control of the Sejm, support for them is still strong in Poland.

What was telling was the voter turnout, which at 74.4 per cent was the highest recorded since the fall of communism, surpassing the records set in 1989 and 2019. Key to the victory of the centre-left was the vote of young people. Turnout for the age group eighteen to twenty-nine reached 68.8 per cent, compared to 46.4 per cent in the previous elections of 2019 (Junes 2023); among these voters, support for Law and Justice fell to 14.9 per cent from 26.3 per cent four years earlier (Szczerbiak 2023). The promise of reversal of Law and Justice's stance on the LGBT community might have been what swung it for young voters: during Civic Platform's campaign Donald Tusk said he would make it a priority to introduce same-sex civil partnerships. He also vowed to legalize abortion up to twelve weeks.

It's no doubt the case that many different factors galvanized young people to vote out Law and Justice. If YouTube comments on 'Polskie Tango' (Polish Tango) are anything to go by, then at least some of his fans attributed the victory to Hemingway, congratulating him on having achieved his mission of defeating the party. Still, within the context of Hemingway's whole discography and the fact that he abandons politics after *Jarmark* (*Fair*), the album can be seen as an experimental anomaly that ultimately failed, if not in the eyes of Hemingway's fans, then certainly in the eyes of his critics and potentially Hemingway himself. Because of this fact, it will likely remain Hemingway's most distinctive album within his body of work. Also because of this – in the opinion of this listener at least – *Jarmark* (*Fair*) is the Taco Hemingway album that deserves the most analysis and ultimately, celebration.

Bibliography

Aniskiewicz, Alena. 'How Polish Hip-Hop Remixed Romanticism'. *Culture.pl*, 2021. https://culture.pl/en/article/how-polish-hip-hop-remixed-romanticism.

Auslander, Philip. *Music in the Twentieth Century*. Cambridge: Cambridge University Press, 2004.

Auslander, Philip. *Performing Glam Rock: Gender and Theatricality in Popular Music*. Michigan: University of Michigan Press, 2006.

Baliński, Jacek and Bartek Strowski. *To nie jest hip-hop. Rozmowy II*. Warsaw: No Dayz Off, 2019.

Bandosz, Benjamin. 'Neoromantic Myths, Modernist Irreverence, and the Gombrowiczean Turn in Polish Hip Hop'. *Canadian Slavonic Papers* 64, no. 1 (2022): 20–41. https://doi.org/10.1080/00085006.2022.2035203

Bartkowski, Dawid. 'PZPN, panie rezyseze. Trójkąt Warszawski – recenzja'. *Goodkid*, 2014. https://goodkid.pl/pzpn-panie-rezyseze-trojkat-warszawski-recenzja/

Beśka, Miłosz. 'Najmniej ciekawy jarmark na jakim byłem – recenzja najnowszej płyty Taco Hemingwaya'. *Sajko*, 2020. https://sajko.network/najmniej-ciekawy-jarmark-recenzja-najnowszej-plyty-taco-hemingwaya/

Böröcz, József. *The European Union and Global Social Change: A Critical Geopolitical-Economic Analysis*. London: Routledge, 2009.

Bosomtwe, Oliwia. 'Taco Hemingway siedzi w Londynie i czyta gazety, ale nie przedstawia żadnej nowej perspektywy'. *Noizz*,

2020. https://noizz.pl/muzyka/recenzujemy-dwa-nowe-albumy-taco-hemingwaya-jarmark-i-europa/w309dve

Boym, Svetlana. *The Future of Nostalgia*. New York: Basic Books, 2001.

Ciepłota, Bartłomiej. 'Taco Hemingway "Jarmark/Europa": populizm goni populizm – recenzja'. *Glamrap*, 2020. https://glamrap.pl/taco-hemingway-jarmark-europa-populizm-goni-populizm-recenzja/

Davies, Norman. *God's Playground: A History of Poland Volume II: 1795 to the Present*. Oxford: Oxford University Press, 1981.

Davies, Norman. *Heart of Europe: A Short History of Poland*. Oxford: Oxford University Press, 1984.

Deditius, Sabina. 'Obelga jako rytuał w rap bitwie'. In *Hip-hop w Polsce. Od blokowisk do kultury popularnej*, edited by Miłosz Miszczyński, 29–57. Warsaw: Wydawnictwa Uniwersytetu Warszawskiego, 2014.

Delaney, Kate and Andrzej Antoszek. 'Americanization and Anti-Americanism in Poland: A Case Study, 1945–2006'. In *Global Perspectives on the United States: Pro-Americanism, Anti-Americanism, and the Discourses Between*, edited by Virginia R. Domínguez, and Jane C. Desmond. 73–91. Champaign, IL: Illinois Scholarship Online, 2017.

Dziewanowski, M. K. *Poland in the Twentieth Century*. New York: Columbia University Press, 1977.

Elavsky, Michael C. 'Musically Mapped: Czech Popular Music as a Second "World Sound"'. *European Journal of Cultural Studies* 14, no. 1 (2011): 3–24.

Eurostat. 'How Much Time Per Week do Europeans Usually Work?' *European Union*, 2023. https://ec.europa.eu/eurostat/web/products-eurostat-news/w/ddn-20230920-1#:~:text=Signi ficant%20differences%20among%20EU%20countries,)%20 and%20Denmark%20(35.4

Flint, Marcin. 'Recenzja Taco Hemingway 'Marmur': Na co ci to, Taco?'. *Interia*, 2016. https://muzyka.interia.pl/recenzje/news-recenzja-taco-hemingway-marmur-na-co-ci-to-taco,nId,2305596

Fosbraey, Glenn. *Reading Eminem: A Critical, Lyrical Analysis*. Cham: Springer, 2022.

Frith, Simon. *Performing Rites: On the Value of Popular Music*. Cambridge, MA: Harvard University Press, 1996.

Gabryszak, Renata. 'The Evolution of the Positions on Social Issues of Major Political Parties in Poland. Comparative Analysis of the Election Programs of Platforma Obywatelska (Civic Platform) and Prawo i Sprawiedliwość (Law and Justice) from 2007, 2011 and 2015.' *Przegląd Politologiczny* no. 4 (2019): 95–108. https://doi.org/10.14746/pp.2019.24.4.7

Galasiński, Dariusz and Aleksandra Galasińska. Lost in Communism, Lost in Migration: Narratives of Post-1989 Polish Migrant Experience. Journal of Multicultural Discourses 2, no. 1 (2007): 47–62.

Galasińska, Aleksandra. 'Gossiping in the Polish Club: An Emotional Coexistence of 'Old' and 'New' Migrants'. *Journal of Ethnic and Migration Studies* 36, no. 6 (2010): 939–51. https://doi.org/10.1080/13691831003643363

Galasińska, Aleksandra and Anna Horolets. 'The (pro)long(ed) Life of a "Grand Narrative": The Case of Internet Forum Discussions on Post-2004 Polish Migration to the United Kingdom'. *Text & Talk* 32, no. 2 (2012): 125–43. https://doi.org/10.1515/text-2012-0007

Grabowska, Izabela. 'Social Remittances: Channels of Diffusion'. In *The Impact of Migration on Poland: EU Mobility and Social Change*, edited by Anne White, Izabela Grabowska, Paweł Kaczmarczyk and Krystyna Slany, 68–89. London: UCL Press, 2018.

Grupa, Hubert. 'Pejzaż'. *Europavox*, 2020. https://www.europavox.com/bands/pejzaz/

Jakub Cebula. *Taco Hemingway - London E1 Koncert 01.12.18 Cafe Belga Tour* [Video]. *YouTube*, 5 December 2018. https://www.youtube.com/watch?v=Ed4Ye-wT3YE

Jamrozik, Żaneta. 'Everything I Love: Sensuous Homelands as a Way of Experiencing History through Hip-Hop Films'. *Studies in Eastern European Cinema*, 7, no. 3 (2016): 208–24. https://doi.org/10.1080/2040350X.2016.1219146

Kleyff, Tomasz. 'Rzut oka wstecz'. In *Antologia Polskiego Rapu*, edited by Dominika Węcławek, Marcin Flint, Tomasz Kleyff, Andrzej Cała, Kamil Jaczyński, 14–23. Warsaw: Narowode Centrum Kultury, 2014.

Junes, Tom. '"No Country for Old Men": How Young Voters Helped Swing the Elections in Poland', *Euronews*, 2023. https://www.euronews.com/2023/10/18/no-country-for-old-men-how-young-voters-helped-swing-the-elections-in-poland

Kapur, Devesh 'The political impact of international migration on sending countries'. Paper Presented at the SSRC Conference on Migration and Development: Future Directions for Research and Policy, New York, 28 February–1 March, 2008.

Kempiński, Grzegorz. 'Pół English, pół polish: czy polskim raperom opłaca się nawijać po angielsku?' *SwipeTo*, 2023. https://swipeto.pl/70312332/polscy-raperzy-nawijajacy-po-angielsku

Kmiecik, Mikołaj. 'Taco Hemingway – "Marmur" | RECENZJA'. *GlamRap*, 2016. https://glamrap.pl/taco-hemingway-marmur-i-recenzja/

Kołodziejczak, Karolina and Katarzyna Smoter. 'Portret polskich millenialsów w twórczości muzycznej Taco Hemingwaya'. *Kultura i Wychowanie* 2, no. 14 (2018): 103–24. https://doi.org/10.25312/2083-2923.14/2018

Konwicki, Tadeusz.. *The Polish Complex*, translated by Richard Lourie. Illinois: Dalkey Archive Press, 1998.

Korycka, Marta. 'Taco Hemingway pierwszym polskim twórcą z miliardem odtworzeń w serwisie Spotify'. *Gazeta.pl*, 2021. https://kultura.gazeta.pl/kultura/7,114526,26952865,taco-hemingway-pierwszym-polskim-tworca-z-miliardem-odtworzen.html.

Krakowski, Krzysztof. 'Disowanie: socjologiczna analiza konfliktów w hip-hopie'. In *Hip-hop w Polsce. Od blokowisk do kultury popularnej*, edited by Miłosz Miszczyński, 58–83. Warsaw: Wydawnictwa Uniwersytetu Warszawskiego, 2014.

Krzyżowski, Łukasz. 'Structuring Social Remittances: Transnational Networks of Polish Migrants'. In *Migration and Social Remittances in a Global Europe*, edited by Magdalena Nowicka, and Vojin Šerbedžija, 71–94. London: Palgrave Macmillan, 2016.

Kukołowicz. Tomasz. 'Pętle, sample i podbicia: techniki kompozycji i struktura Utworu hip-hopowego'. In *Hip-hop w Polsce. Od blokowisk do kultury popularnej*, edited by Miłosz Miszczyński, 21–38. Warsaw: Wydawnictwa Uniwersytetu Warszawskiego, 2014.

kultura niska. *RECENZJA: Taco Hemingway - Jarmark (2020)* [Video]. *YouTube*, 13 October 2020. https://www.youtube.com/watch?app=desktop&v=Blnv2-_HMnk

Kurnicki, Karol. 'Dziś w moim mieście". Społeczna i polityczna przestrzeń codzienna w hip-hopie'. In *Hip-hop w Polsce. Od blokowisk do kultury popularnej*, edited by Miłosz Miszczyński, 144–64. Warsaw: Wydawnictwa Uniwersytetu Warszawskiego, 2014.

Lech, Filip. 'The Best of Early Polish Hip-Hop: 1995-2002'. *Culture.pl*, 2023. https://culture.pl/en/article/the-best-of-early-polish-hip-hop-1995-2002

Lekko Stronniczy. *Taco Hemingway: Jarmark. Co poszło nie tak? Szczera opinia. - Lekko Stronniczy* [Video]. *YouTube*, 2 September 2020. https://www.youtube.com/watch?v=oljb5trJF3U

Levitt, Peggy. 'Social Remittances: Migration Driven Local-Level Forms of Cultural Diffusion'. *The International Migration Review* 32, no. 4 (1998): 926–48. https://doi.org/10.2307/2547666

Levitt, Peggy and Deepak Lamba-Nieves. 'Social Remittances Revisited'. *Journal of Ethnic and Migration Studies* 37, no. 1 (2011): 1–22. https://doi.org/10.1080/1369183X.2011.521361

Lukowski, Jerzy and Hubert Zawadzki. *A Concise History of Poland*. Cambridge: Cambridge University Press, 2019.

Majewski, Piotr. 'African-American Music in the Service of White Nationalists: Polish "Patriotic Rap" as a Pop Cultural Tool to Promote National Values'. *European Journal of American Studies* 13, no. 3 (2018): 1–18. https://doi.org/10.4000/ejas.13655

Marshall, Alex. 'A Rap Star Agonizes About His Role in Poland's Culture Wars'. *The New York Times*, 2020. https://www.nytimes.com/2020/10/30/arts/music/taco-hemingway-poland-rap.html

Mastalski, Arkadiusz S. 'Rap jako rodzaj współczesnej melorecytacji'. In *Hip-hop w Polsce. Od blokowisk do kultury popularnej*, edited by Miłosz Miszczyński, 105–23. Warsaw: Wydawnictwa Uniwersytetu Warszawskiego, 2014.

Mazierska, Ewa. 'From Self-colonisation to Conquest in Eastern European Postcommunist Musicals'. *Studies in European Cinema* 20, no. 3 (2023a): 306–23. https://doi.org/10.1080/17411548.2022.2031806

Mazierska, Ewa. 'Introduction'. In *Popular Music in Eastern Europe*, edited by Ewa Mazierska, 1–27. London: Palgrave Macmillan, 2016.

Mazierska, Ewa. *Polish Estrada Music: Organisation, Stars and Representation*, 1st edn. New York: Routledge, 2023b. https://doi-org.manchester.idm.oclc.org/10.4324/9781003198536

Mazierska, Ewa. 'Representation of Poverty and Precarity in Post-Communist Polish Cinema'. In *Precarity in European Film*, edited by Elisa Cuter, Guido Kirsten and Hanna Prenzel, 271–87. Berlin, Boston: De Gruyter, 2022.

Mazierska, Ewa, Lars Lyngsgaard Fjord Kristensen and Eva Näripea. 'Postcolonial Theory and the Postcommunist World'. In *Postcolonial Approaches to Eastern European Cinema : Portraying Neighbours on-Screen*, edited by Ewa Mazierska, Lars Kristensen and Eva Näripea, 1–40. London: I.B. Tauris, 2014.

Mazierska, Ewa and Michael Goddard. 'Polish Cinema beyond Polish Borders'. In *Cinema in a Transnational Context*, edited by Ewa Mazierska and Michael Goddard, 1–22. Rochester, NY: University of Rochester Press, 2014.

Mezzadra, Sandro and Brett Neilson. *Border as Method, or, the Multiplication of Labor*. Durham, NC: Duke University Press, 2013.

Middleton, Richard. *Voicing the Popular: On the Subjects of Popular Music*, 1st edn. New York: Routledge, 2006. https://doi-org.manchester.idm.oclc.org/10.4324/9780203036228

Miszczynski, Milosz and Adriana Helbig. 'Introduction'. In *Hip Hop at Europe's Edge: Music, Agency, and Social Change*, edited by Milosz Miszczynski and Adriana Helbig, 1–8. Indiana: Indiana University Press, 2017. https://doi.org/10.2307/j.ctt2005sm8.

Miszczynski, Milosz and Przemyslaw Tomaszewski. 'Wearing Nikes for a Reason: A Critical Analysis of Brand Usage in Polish Rap'. In *Hip Hop at Europe's Edge: Music, Agency and Social Chance*, edited by Adriana Helbig and Milosz Miszczynski, 145–62. Bloomington: Indiana University Press, 2017.

Mrożek, Sławomir. *Striptease; Tango; Vatzlav: Three Plays*. New York: Grove Press, 1981.

Muzyk. 'Polskie Tango – Taco Hemingway przebił samego siebie'. *Muzyk*, 2020. https://muzyk.net/polskie-tango-taco-hemingway-przebil-samego-siebie/

Nazaruk, Igor. 'Taco Hemingway: 'Trójkąt warszawski' jest o pijanych, zakochanych ludziach w mieście [WYWIAD]'. *Gazeta.pl*, 2015. https://metrowarszawa.gazeta.pl/metrowarszawa/7,141635,17541734,taco-hemingway-trojkat-warszawski-jest-o-pijanych-zakochanych.html

Niemietz, Kristian. *Left turn ahead: Surveying attitudes of young people towards capitalism and socialism*. London: Institute of Economic Affairs, 2021. https://iea.org.uk/wp-content/uploads/2021/07/Left-turn-ahead.pdf

Nirav Ractions. *Taco Hemingway - POLSKIE TANGO (Angielska reakcja) [With English Subtitles]* [Video]. *YouTube*, 10 July 2020. https://www.youtube.com/watch?v=7koDZGH6iC4

North, Douglass C. *Understanding the Process of Economic Change*. Princeton, Oxford: Princeton University Press, 2005.

Nowak, Andrzej W. 'Fear, Doubt and Money. War of Ideas, Production of Ignorance and Right-Wing Infrastructures of Knowledge and Hegemony in Poland'. In *The Political Economy of Eastern Europe 30 years into the 'Transition'*, edited by Agnes Gagyi and Ondřej Slačálek, 223–50. Cham: Palgrave Macmillan, 2022.

Oleksiak, Olga. 'Taco Hemingway: okładka Jarmarku to plagiat? Jest oświadczenie'. *4fun.tv*, 2020. https://4fun.tv/news/taco-hemingway-jarmark-okladka-plagiat-oswiadczenie-alex-prager

Okólski, M. 'Incomplete Migration: A New Form of Mobility in Central and Eastern Europe. The Case of Polish and Ukrainian Migrants'. In *Patterns of Migration in Central Europe*, edited by C. Wallace and D. Stola, 105–28. London: Palgrave Macmillan. 2001.

Orliński, Wojciech. 'Power and Catholicism were Inseparable in Poland. The Fall of Populists Mirrors that of Priests'. *Guardian*, 2023. https://www.theguardian.com/commentisfree/2023/nov/10/poland-power-catholicism-church-left-parties.

Page, Will and Chris Dalla Riva. '"Glocalisation" of Music Streaming within and across Europe'. Europe in Question. *London School of Economics and Political Science*, 2023. https://www.lse.ac.uk/european-institute/Assets/Documents/LEQS-Discussion-Papers/EIQPaper182.pdf

Pasternak-Mazur, Renata. 'The Black Muse: Polish Hip-Hop as the Voice of "New Others" in the Post-Socialist Transition'. *Music and Politics* 3, no. 1 (2009): 1–18. https://doi.org/10.3998/mp.9460447.0003.103

Pawlak, Renata. *Polska kultura hip-hopowa*. Kagra Krzysztof Grausz, 2004.

Perdał, Robert. 'Geographical and Historical Background of the Transformation: Politics and Society'. In *Three Decades of Polish Socio-economic Transformations*, Economic Geography, edited by Paweł Churski and Tomasz Kaczmarek, 37–80. Cham: Springer, 2022.

Pew Research Center. 'Modest Declines in Positive Views of "Socialism" and "Capitalism" in U.S'. *Pew Research Centre*, 2022. https://www.pewresearch.org/wp-content/uploads/sites/20/2022/09/PP_2022.09.19_socialism-capitalism_REPORT.pdf

Regev, Motti. *Pop-Rock Music: Aesthetic Cosmopolitanism in Late Modernity*. Cambridge: Polity, 2013.

Regev, Motti. 'The Pop-Rockization of Popular Music'. In *Popular Music Studies*, edited by David Hesmondhalgh and Keith Negus, 251–64. London: Arnold, 2002.

Reuters. 'Police Raid Largest Amphetamine Factory Ever Found in Poland'. *Reuters*, 2014. https://www.reuters.com/article/poland-drugs/police-raid-largest-amphetamine-factory-ever-found-in-poland-idUKL5N0MM2OG20140325/

Rymajdo, Kamila. 'Polish Music in British Nightclubs: Examining How Nostalgic Longing Brought Disco Polo and Polish

Hip-Hop to the United Kingdom'. In *Made in Poland*, edited by Patryk Galuszka, 189–200. New York: Routledge, 2019.

Rymajdo, Kamila. 'Polski Riddim: Meet the Polish MCs Making Grime in the UK'. *Vice*, 2016. https://www.vice.com/en/article/rze5p8/polish-hip-hop-in-the-united-kingdom

Rollefson, J. Griffith. *Flip the Script: European Hip Hop and the Politics of Postcoloniality*. Chicago and London: The University of Chicago Press, 2017.

Sabater, Albert. 'Between Flows and Places: Using Geodemographics to Explore EU Migration across Neighbourhoods in Britain'. *European Journal of Population* 31 (2015): 207–30. https://doi.org/10.1007/s10680-015-9344-2

Sadowski, Ireneusz and Bogdan W. Mach. 'Is the "Third Generation" of the Polish Transformation More Economically Liberal? Inter-Cohort Differences in Job Entrance and Egalitarian Attitudes'. *Polish Sociological Review 2021* 213, no. 1 (2021): 3–26. https://doi.org/10.26412/psr213.01

Sadowski, Robert. 'Newspoint Report: Generations in Poland and the Need to Monitor their Growing Activity'. *Newspoint.pl*, 2018. https://www.newspoint.pl/en/blog/newspoint-report-generations-in-poland-and-the-need-to-monitor-their-growing-activity

Samaluk, Barbara. 'Migration, Consumption and Work: A Postcolonial Perspective on Post-socialist Migration to the UK'. E*phemera: Theory & Politics in Organization* 16, no. 3 (2016): 95–118. www.ephemerajournal.org/sites/default/files/ pdfs/contribution/16-3samaluk.pdf.

Samborski, Rafał. 'Taco Hemingway "Jarmark": Dozwolone do lat 18 [RECENZJA]'. *Interia*, 2020. https://muzyka.interia.pl/recenzje/news-taco-hemingway-jarmark-dozwolone-do-lat-18-recenzja,nId,4709108#google_vignette

Samborski, Rafał. 'Taco Hemingway 'Pocztówka z WWA, LATO "19": Letnia składanka [RECENZJA]'. *Interia*, 2019. https://muzyka.interia.pl/recenzje/news-taco-hemingway-pocztowka-z-wwa-lato-19-letnia-skladanka-rece,nId,3117413

Solomon, Thomas. 'Berlin–Frankfurt–Istanbul: Turkish Hip-Hop in Motion'. *European Journal of Cultural Studies* 12, no. 3 (2009): 305–27. https://doi.org/10.1177/1367549409105366

Soundcharts. *Taco Hemingway*. Soundcharts, 14 February 2024. https://app.soundcharts.com/app/artist/taco-hemingway/overview

Spotify. 'Celebrating 10 Years of Spotify in Italy and Poland'. *Spotify*, 2023. https://newsroom.spotify.com/2023-03-01/celebrating-10-years-of-spotify-in-italy-and-poland/#:~:text=Looking%20back%2C%20international%20artists%20controlled,Podsiad%C5%82o%20took%20the%20top%20spots.

Spotify. *Taco Hemingway*. Spotify, 14 February 2024. https://open.spotify.com/artist/7CJgLPEqilRuneZSolpawQ

Stackiewicz, Izabela. 'Taco Hemingway z nowym krążkiem "Marmur" wita w Hotelu Marmur'. *wPolityce*, 2016. https://wpolityce.pl/kultura/317545-taco-hemingway-z-nowym-krazkiem-marmur-wita-w-hotelu-marmur

Szarecki, Artur. 'The Making of Polish Hip-Hop'. In *Made in Poland*, edited by Patryk Galuszka, 155–64. New York: Routledge, 2019.

Szczerbiak, Aleks. 'Why did the Opposition Win the Polish Election?' *LSE Blogs*, 2023. https://blogs.lse.ac.uk/europpblog/2023/11/02/why-did-the-opposition-win-the-polish-election/

Szufladowicz, Kamil. 'Borucci: kiedyś nagrałem cały projekt z Taco, ale nigdy nie został wydany (ROZMOWA)'. *Newonce*, 2020a. https://newonce.net/artykul/borucci-kiedys-nagralem-cay-projekt-z-taco-ale-nigdy-nie-zosta-wydany-rozmowa

Szufladowicz, Kamil. 'The one and only na fonii - którzy polscy raperzy używają najwięcej anglicyzmów?' *Newonce*, 2020b. https://newonce.net/artykul/the-one-and-only-na-fonii-czyli-jezyk-angielski-w-polskim-rapie

Tracz, Jan. 'Taco ostro o wychowaniu na pornografii i influencerach. "Jarmark" to album pełen przeciwieństw'. *Noizz*, 2020. https://noizz.pl/muzyka/porno-i-influencerzy-recenzja-najnowszej-plyty-taco-hemingwaya-jarmark/rbe1vj5.

Uniwersum Dźwięku. 'Trójkąt Warszawski'. *Uniwersum Dźwięku*, 2014. https://sounduniverse.pl/recenzje/trojkat-warszawski/

V-nesh. *Taco Hemingway - POLSKIE TANGO (w English Translation) | POLISH RAP REACTION* [Video]. *YouTube*, 15 July 2020. https://www.youtube.com/watch?v=-FkQaTKUmpk

Ventsel, Arman. 'Estonian Invasion as Western Ersatz Pop'. In *Popular Music in Eastern Europe*, edited by Ewa Mazierska. 69–88. London: Palgrave Macmillan, 2016.

Wallis, Roger and Krister Malm. *Big Sounds From Small Peoples: the Music Industry in Small Countries*. London: Constable, 1984.

Wernio, Maciej. 'Taco Hemingway vs polscy raperzy. Niby "rap dla dziewczynek", ale wielu mogłoby się od niego uczyć'. *Noizz*, 2017. https://noizz.pl/muzyka/taco-hemingway-vs-polscy-raperzy-niby-rap-dla-dziewczynek-ale-wielu-mogloby-sie-od/5f3zb7n

Wernio, Maciej. 'Taco Hemingway zapowiada swój nowy projekt pierwszym singlem. Narzekaliście, że raper rzadko angażuje się w sprawy polityczne i społeczne albo że brakuje mu agresji w numerach? Zapraszamy na "Polskie Tango"'. *Noizz*, 2020. https://noizz.pl/muzyka/taco-hemingway-zapowiada-plyte-singlem-polskie-tango/hrll7vn

White, Anne, Izabela Grabowska, Paweł Kaczmarczyk and Krystyna Slany. 2018. 'The Impact of Migration from and to Poland since EU Accession'. In *The Impact of Migration on*

Poland: EU Mobility and Social Change, edited by Anne White, Izabela Grabowska, Paweł Kaczmarczyk and Krystyna Slany, 10–41. London: UCL Press, 2018.

Wójtowicz, Stanisław. 'O kierunkach w polskich badaniach literaturoznawczych nad hip-hopem'. In *Hip-hop w Polsce. Od blokowisk do kultury popularnej*, edited by Miłosz Miszczyński, 183–98. Warsaw: Wydawnictwa Uniwersytetu Warszawskiego, 2014.

Wolniaczyk, Klaudia and Maciek Piasecki. 'Dlaczego ludzie jarają się Taco Hemingwayem?' *Vice*, 2015. https://www.vice.com/pl/article/bn9xmz/dlaczego-ludzie-jaraja-sie-taco-hemingwayem

Zbytniewska, Karolina. 'Populist Skirmishers: Frontrunners of Populist Radical Right in Poland'. *Politics and Governance* 10, no. 4 (2022): 72–83. https://doi.org/10.17645/pag.v10i4.5585

Index

'+4822' 31
1-800-Oświecenie
	(*1-800-Enlightenment*)
	27, 102–3
'6 zer' (6 zeros) 41, 81
'8 kobiet' (8 women) 94
'100 km/h' 94
500+ child benefit 90
'1990s Utopia' 51, 70, 72, 90–1, 97
'2031' 44
'900729' 40

abortion law 22–4, 106
Asfalt Records 26
'Awizo' (Advice) 31

Bedoes 14, 51, 93, 96
Białas 51
Biggie Smalls 48
'Bigos' (Hunter's stew) 96
'Big Pharma' 94
Blokersi (film) 19
Borucci 28, 51, 81

Café Belga 27, 44–5, 98
capitalism/capitalist 5–6, 11–12, 16, 19, 53–5, 60, 67, 68, 70, 72–3, 76, 77, 95
CatchUp 51
Catholic Church 22–3, 25, 51, 57, 67, 70, 78, 90
'Chłopaki nie płaczą' (Boys don't cry) 93
Civic Coalition 105
Civic Platform 21, 106
club2020 101, 103
Coals 51, 70, 97
Cold War 2, 38
colonialism 77–8
communism 2, 5, 15, 17, 23, 30, 39, 53, 56, 59, 61, 79–80, 84, 106

Dawid, Leszek 9, 19
'Deszcz na betonie' (Rain on concrete) 43
disco polo 6, 83
Drake 2, 48, 68, 81

Duda, Andrzej   49, 97
'Dwuzłotówki Dancing' (Two-Zloty Coins Dancing)   50, 67–70

Eastern Bloc   78
Eldo   7, 19
Europa (*Europe*)   27, 41–2, 45, 50, 53, 85, 92–4, 100, 102
European hip hop/rap   2, 4, 10, 15, 34–5
European Union (EU)   1, 5, 9, 17–18, 22, 25, 30–1, 37–8, 42, 53, 79, 91–2, 105
   enlargement   1, 5

Flagey   27, 45
Foodvillain   25
Fryderyk award   27, 49, 87, 94, 102
Future   68, 81

gangsta rap   5, 7, 12, 29, 46
Gen Z   33–4, 95–6, 101
Globalization   11, 19, 84
Gombrowicz, Witold   44
Grammatik   7, 19
Grand Narrative   38–9, 47, 87, 96, 100
The Great Emigration   36–7

Hemingway, Ernest   26
hip-hopolo   8, 41
'Influenza'   51, 73

Iron Curtain   15, 18, 23, 53

Jarmark Europa   53
Jesteś Bogiem (*You Are God*)   9, 19

Kaliber 44   8, 13
Kowalczyk, Katarzyna   51, 70, 97
'Kryptowaluty' (Cryptocurrencies)   45
'Kurtz'   48

'Łańcuch' (Chain) trilogy   51, 59, 62, 75–6, 97
'Łańcuch I: Kiosk' (Chain I: Kiosk)   50, 59, 90
'Łańcuch II: Korek' (Chain II: Traffic Jam)   50, 61
'Łańcuch III: Korpo' (Chain: Corpo)   50, 61
Law and Justice   20–2, 24–5, 49, 51, 57, 74, 89–92, 97, 105–6
League of Polish Families   20, 84

LGBT 22, 57, 92, 105–6
Liroy 5, 80
'Luxembourg' 41

market democracy 53, 62, 73–4, 80
 economy 16, 30–1
Marmur (*Marble*) 27–8, 40–3, 94, 96
'Marsz, marsz' (March, march) 32, 39
Mata 30, 48, 101
Mazowiecki, Tadeusz 16, 23
MF DOOM 26, 48
'Michael Essien Birthday Party' (Michael Essien's Birthday Party) 50
Mickiewicz, Adam 3, 12–13, 24, 36
migration 3–4, 9, 15, 17, 22, 34–9, 41–2, 44, 47, 87–8, 96, 100
millennials 25, 29–34, 39, 73, 95
Młody Matczak (*Young Matczak*) 48, 101
Molesta 6–8
'A mówiłem Ci' (I told you so) 40
Mrożek, Sławomir 54, 61
musical personas 46–7

'Na Paryskie Getto Pada Deszcz' (It's Raining on a Paris Ghetto) 46
Nas 45, 48, 52
neoliberal 20, 22, 93
'Nie Mam Czasu' (I Don't Have Time) 50, 73
Niemen, Czesław 37, 102
Norwid, Cyprian 37, 41, 100

O.S.T.R. 7, 24
'Od zera' (From zero) 41
'Ortalion' (Nylon) 45–6

Paktofonika 7, 19, 20
'Panie, to Wyście!' (Sir, it's You!) 51, 57, 64, 92
patriotic rap 25
Peja 6–7, 12, 19, 24
Pejzaż 51, 70
Pocztówka z Polski Tour (*Postcard from Poland Tour*) 48
POCZTÓWKA Z WWA, LATO '19 (*POSTCARD FROM WWA, SUMMER '19*) 49, 98
Podsiadło, Dawid 28–9, 103
poetic devices 52, 63, 70, 76
'Pokédex' 45
Polish Film Chronicle 53, 66
Polish Romanticism 13, 23, 36–7, 41, 44

'Polskie Tango' (Polish Tango) 27, 29, 49, 51, 53–6, 61, 76, 90–1, 97, 99, 105–6
'POL Smoke' 51, 81, 99
populist turn 15, 51, 52, 84
postcolonialism 3, 15, 35, 52
postsocialist 9–11, 15, 51, 55

Quebonafide 27, 29, 45, 94, 103

Rojek, Artur 28, 49, 51, 60, 85
Ruch Ośmiu Gwiazd 91
Rumak 26, 28, 50

Schafter 13, 96
Second World War 36–7
Self Defence 20, 84
Skepta 2, 45, 48
'Ślepe sumy' (Blind sums) 94
Słowacki, Juliusz 13, 36–7
Slums Attack 6, 19
socialism 9, 16–17, 53, 80, 83
social remittances 4, 87–9, 92, 96
Solidarity 16–17, 23, 30
Soma 0,5 mg 27, 94
Soviet Bloc 9, 79

Soviet Union 10, 100
Stadion Dziesięciolecia (10th-Anniversary Stadium) 53, 82–3
'Świat jest WFem' (The world is like PE) 40
'Szczękościsk' (Lockjaw) 50, 73–4
'Szlugi i kalafiory' (Fags and cauliflowers) 33
'Sznycel' (Schnitzel) 50–51
Szprycer (Spritzer) 27–8
'Sztylet' (Dagger) 42, 45

Taco Corp 50
Taconafide 27, 29, 103
'Tamagotchi' 45
Tango 54, 61
'Toskania Outro' (Tuscany Outro) 93
A Tribe Called Quest 80, 82
Trójkąt warszawski (Warsaw triangle) 1, 26, 31–3, 39–42, 50, 96
Tusk, Donald 105–6

uliczny hip hop 6, 12
Umowa o dzieło (Contract work) 27, 31, 40, 94, 96
United Kingdom 1, 7, 9, 37, 41, 47–8, 95

USSR   23, 36, 78

Wałęsa, Lech   16, 20
West, Kanye   28, 48, 52, 81
Who Killed JFK   26
'Wiatr' (Wind)   81
Wosk (*Wax*)   27, 81, 89
'W PIĄTKI LEŻĘ W WANNIE' (ON FRIDAYS I LIE IN THE BATH)   49

'Wszystko jedno' (Doesn't matter)   32
'WWA Nie Berlin' (WWA Not Berlin)   92
'Wychowała Nas Pornografia' (Pornography Raised Us)   51, 74, 91

Young Hems   26

Zipera   7, 24
'Żyrandol' (Chandelier)   43
'Żywot' (Life)   40–1